THE HOOKUP HANDBOOK

A Single Girl's Guide to Living It Up

Andrea Lavinthal and Jessica Rozler

Illustrations by Cindy Luu

SIMON SPOTLIGHT ENTERTAINMENT

New York London Toronto Sydney

SIMON SPOTLIGHT ENTERTAINMENT
An imprint of Simon & Schuster
1230 Avenue of the Americas, New York, New York 10020
Text copyright © 2005 by Andrea Lavinthal and Jessica Rozler
Illustrations copyright © 2005 by Cindy Luu
SIMON SPOTLIGHT ENTERTAINMENT and related logo are trademarks
of Simon & Schuster, Inc.
Book designed by Joel Avirom and Jason Snyder
Manufactured in the United States of America
First Edition 10 9 8 7 6 5 4 3 2 1
Library of Congress Cataloging-in-Publication Data
Lavinthal, Andrea.
The hookup handbook : a single girl's guide to living it up /
Andrea Lavinthal and Jessica Rozler ; illustrations by Cindy Luu.—1st ed.
p. cm.
ISBN 0-689-87646-7
1. Dating (Social customs) 2. Man-woman relationships.
I. Rozler, Jessica. II. Luu, Cindy. III. Title.
HQ801.L335 2005
646.7'7—dc22
2004014052

For every girl who lives life
by her own rules—not *The Rules*

ACKNOWLEDGMENTS

We'd like to thank our fab editor at Simon Spotlight Entertainment, Elizabeth Bracken, for guiding us through the uncharted waters of writing our first book. You rock! Thanks to Trish Boczkowski and Patrick Price for bringing us on board, and to Micol Ostow for getting the whole ball rolling on this project. Thanks to Cindy Luu for her great illustrations too.

We'd also like to thank our moms, dads, and big brothers, Adam and Joel, for their love, support, and inspiration.

Thanks to our profs at the Newhouse School for letting us know that you don't need to write about important stuff like politics, war, and J.Lo to be considered esteemed journalists.

Of course, thank you to all of our friends, friends of friends, and friends of friends of friends who allowed us to pry into their personal lives so we could hear their stories. Without your collective experiences, this book wouldn't be as funny—or as true. Thank you for reading and rereading all our stuff.

A very special thanks to our agent, Adam Chromy of Artists and Artisans Inc., for thinking that we were actually funny and taking a chance on us.

Thank you to the boys, too. Especially Bad Hair Boy. You know who you are.

CONTENTS

PART III **THE MORNING AFTER**
What Happens When the Buzz Wears Off

INTRODUCTION
A Casual Affair

t's not sex and the city—it's sex and your city, your bedroom, your dorm room, or anywhere else two people get it on. Or maybe it isn't sex at all. Maybe it's kissing, making out, or getting to third base. One thing's for sure: It's not a one-night stand, it's not dating, and it's not jamming your foot into a teeny glass slipper in the hopes that you'll one day marry a Prince Charming who can support you in the princess lifestyle to which you hope to become accustomed.

It's "hooking up," the vague phrase used to describe what happens between two people who don't necessarily have any foreseeable future or even a hint of commitment. Hooking up is a bunch of things (or it isn't, depending on whom you ask). What we do know is that it has become the most accepted term for our generation's extracurricular activities. We remember first hearing it when we were in high school, but since then it's cast its commitment-phobic net onto college and beyond.

Yes, the rules have changed. Way back in the day, when Brazilian bikini waxes were reserved for strippers and Brazilians, and mobile phones could easily double as free weights, the term "hooking up" didn't even exist. Instead, a girl often found herself asking: "When do you think he'll call?"; "It's been three dates, should I sleep with him?"; or "Should I take him home to meet my parents?" Today we're more likely to hear: "When do you think he'll call—before or after *last* call?"; "We've hooked up three times, shouldn't he ask me out?"; or "Is it still considered the walk of shame if I take a taxi home?"

If you're unfamiliar with the term "hooking up," maybe this typical scenario will help:

○ Girl A sort of knows Boy B (maybe they were in the same Psych 101 class, have mutual friends, or perhaps they've even slept together before).

- Girl A goes out to the bar with her friends, and Boy B goes out to the bar with his friends.

- Girl A stands in one corner of the bar, downs cosmopolitans, screams the words to "Like a Prayer" at the top of her lungs, and pretends to ignore Boy B.

- Boy B stands in another corner of the bar and chugs beers with his friends.

- When Girl A finally gets enough courage (i.e., is drunk enough), she approaches Boy B and says, "Hey, what's going on?"

- When Boy B finally realizes that Girl A is the best he's going to do tonight, he answers, "Nothin'."

- The two proceed to make out at the bar and then go back to his place and "hook up."

Confused about whether Girl A and Boy B slept together, merely cuddled on the couch, or did some major rewiring of Boy B's home entertainment system? You are not alone. *Ambiguity is key to hooking up.* We've heard it defined as everything from making out to full-on sex, but for most people it's somewhere in between a peck on the lips and some grinding with your hips.

Or, as one of our male friends articulately put it, "It's not hooking up unless I blow my load."

And, while according to Amazon.com (as of the writing of this book), there are 22,395 books about sex, 1,985 books about dating, and 25,652 books about tricking some poor schmuck into marrying you, the only book we could find about hooking up taught us how to effectively design steam systems.[1]

It seems we are part of the dawn of a new era. Dating as we know it has gone the way of dinosaurs, eight-track players, and stirrup pants. Extinct. Vanished. Kaput. Left in its place stand two mighty opponents. In one corner, wearing matching sweats and snuggled together watching Friday-night prime-time TV, we have the "Serious Couple." In the other corner, clad in his-and-hers Seven jeans and armed with open bar tabs, we have the "Hookup." By the looks of things, hooking up is the new heavyweight champion.

So even though hooking up is a national phenomenon whose popularity rivals the height of slap-bracelet fervor, the "it" phrase of single people everywhere has been left unexamined. That's where we come in: We're young, we've lived through the dawn of the hookup, and we've witnessed its reign everywhere from the

---

[1] Next time you're at the beach, don't forget to bring along *Hook-Ups: Design of Fluid Systems*. It's sort of like Jackie Collins meets Bob Vila.

sex-crazed campus of Syracuse University to the bars and clubs of New York City. We've endured endless dinners with our girlfriends where we dissected, analyzed, and discussed their (and our) current hookups. We've sat through countless morning-after brunches listening to the details of the previous night's hookups while trying not to lose our appetite. And we've heard "So, last night we hooked up . . ." so many times that we're now left wondering if that meant they had sex, swapped spit, or just watched the Food Network for a few hours while holding hands.

After months of investigation and years of observation, we've uncovered that while, like snowflakes, no two hookups are identical, there are enough recurring stories to identify fourteen types of these encounters with the opposite sex. But before we get to the good stuff, we had to ask how hooking up became the phenomenon that it is today. No one knows where the term came from, but our best guess is that it evolved from the more casual meaning of "getting together as friends." Here's a helpful time line (it's short, for all you readers with attention deficit issues) of the historical milestones that probably helped squeeze the life out of traditional dating.

A SHORT TIME LINE OF RECENT EVENTS THAT PAVED THE WAY TO A HOOKUP NATION

1956: Elvis swivels his hips on national television and makes the squares all hot and bothered. Teenagers know better: Maybe it's time to toss away the Donna Reed pearls and get a little wild.

1960: The U.S. Food and Drug Administration approves the birth control pill—finally, an alternative to the tried-and-true rhythm method.

1969: Woodstock brings thousands of hippies to upstate New York for peace, tree-smoking, and, of course, free love. Some things never change (except maybe the peace thing).

1971: Oberlin College in Ohio, the nation's first coeducational college, also becomes one of the first schools to permit coed dorms, allowing for easier access to booty.

1977: Studio 54 opens its doors, quickly becoming a haven for public grinding among the rich and fabulous (which was nothing compared to your office holiday party, but still, it was scandalous).

1981: MTV first hits the airwaves. Not a big deal at first, but it eventually gives the nation glimpses of a gyrating Madonna, kinky Prince, and, um, very naughty George Michael (and let's not forget *The Real World*), turning the temperature way up on American pop culture.

1983: Motorola markets the first portable cellular phone for consumers (weighing in at twenty-eight ounces). This little breakthrough opened up the possibility for the first mobile booty calls.

1985: AOL launches, paving the way for cyber-hookups and the ever-popular human-contact eliminator, the instant messenger. By 1994 over one million people were members, and by 2002 everyone was somehow involved in an Internet sex scandal.

1990: Salt-N-Pepa releases the pivotal album *Blacks' Magic*, which contains the safe-sex anthem "Let's Talk About Sex."

1993: The Reality Female Condom gets the go-ahead from the FDA and before long manages to gross out an entire nation.

1998: President Bill Clinton gets caught in a very compromising position with his intern. When he's forced to go public with his extracurricular activities, we get a taste of the first-ever instance of selective storytelling at the White House.

2001: Smirnoff Ice first shows up in bars across the country (not the first premium malt beverage, but much less pathetic than Zima). Finally, even the wusses could get drunk and lower their standards.

2003 AND BEYOND: Recent popular song titles: "Dirrty" and "Magic Stick." Enough said.

In addition to the chronology of it all, we also identified the more general "Big Four" societal symptoms—we like to think of them as enablers—that help explain this growing trend of choosing McBooty over happily ever after. Here is the incriminating evidence (drumroll, please):

EXHIBIT A
Too-Busy-to-Have-a-Boyfriend Syndrome

In between climbing the corporate ladder; bonding with your girlfriends; going to the gym; reading this month's book club pick; staying abreast of the hottest TV shows, movies, and diets; and deciding whether or not to cut bangs; there is little time to devote to having an actual boyfriend. They need to be trained, fed, walked, and played with constantly. Just think how well you took care of your lucky bamboo plant—it didn't look so lucky when you forgot to water it and it shriveled up into what looked like a Slim Jim, right?

EXHIBIT B
Defensive Nondating

This is an uncertain world, where feelings are hurt, hearts are broken, and otherwise savvy chicks are duped into thinking some loser boy really likes them. So eventually you realize (like an Oprah "AHA! moment") that a relationship isn't the easiest thing to obtain, but swearing off boys isn't a viable option either. The result of this epiphany: You refuse to put yourself out there. Instead, you just put out. It may sound slutty, but when you remove the emotional from the physical, you end up making out with a cute boy without the whole "Where is this going?" agony.

EXHIBIT C
Let's Talk About Text, Baby

Ask yourself this: "How did people hook up without cell phones?" As far as we're concerned, that question is up there with "What happened to Jimmy Hoffa's body?" or "Is Tupac really dead?" Unless you were actually there to experience it firsthand, pre–cell phone hooking up remains an unsolvable mystery that is tainted by outlandish theories.[2] The bottom line is that if we didn't have these instant forms of communication (like text messages and IM), hooking up would be dating because you'd actually have to put more than just minimal effort into making something happen.

In case you didn't get the memo, here's the communication breakdown:

- **Text messaging is the new phone call.**
- **IM is the new face-to-face conversation.**
- **Caller ID is the new *69.**

[2] For instance, maybe the guy had to climb into his Corvette and booty call you from his $20-per-minute car phone.

WARNING: Even though cell phones are a surefire path to hooking up, they are not foolproof, because his caller ID will pretty much give you away every time. Just remember this motto: *Straight to voice mail, you're in luck; if it rings even once, you're totally fucked.*

EXHIBIT D
Alcohol, the Not-So-Secret Ingredient in a Hookup

We all know the basics about drinking: It can make you lose your inhibitions, your money, and your standards. So it's no surprise that brews and bubbly are huge players in the hookup game. Here are some other reasons why "drunken" and "hookup" are often uttered together in the same sentence:

- Because grande skim extra foam cappuccinos rarely put people in the mood to get it on

- Because it's kind of awkward to suddenly start making out with a friend of a friend of a friend unless you've been drinking

- Because juicy hookup stories rarely begin with, "So I was completely sober and . . ."

- Because otherwise you might care that the guy you're making out with has a lisp

- Because how else can you explain the eighteen missed calls on his cell phone from 1:32 A.M. to 2:46 A.M.?

- Because booze makes him hotter, taller, and smarter

- Because there's a reason they don't call it "sad hour"

- Because a kiss is just a kiss, but a drunken kiss is entertainment for all of your friends

Based on the impact that the above four factors have had on opposite-sex interaction, it seems to us that dating has evolved from an ancient mating dance into a down-and-dirty booty shake. We call it Relationship Darwinism: Only the strong survive, and in this case, the strong heartily hook up.

Now that you're armed with the facts, we present you with *The Hookup Handbook*. We hope you will find it delicious, informative, and hilarious. After all, this isn't about following a set of rules to find a husband, cutting carbs to whittle down your waist, or donning a tiara and proclaiming that you're the reigning princess of your studio apartment. This is about what single girls are doing right now. And right now, we'd like you to buy us another round.

POP QUIZ
What's Your Hookup Style?

We know you needed a Kaplan class to get you through the SATs, but fear not: There are no wrong answers here.

1. I hook up:

    a. every once in a while. Who doesn't?

    b. my DVD player to my TV.

    c. only on days that end in "y."

2. I wear thongs:

    a. on my feet.

    b. when I don't want visible panty lines.

    c. when I'm lucky enough to find them on the floor the next morning.

3. My longest relationship lasted for:

    a. six months.

    b. six years.

    c. six beers.

4. True or false: Drink till he's cute.

5. If variety is the spice of life, then my romantic life is:

    a. curry.

    b. white rice.

    c. wasabi smeared onto a paper cut.

6. True or false: Manolo Blahniks.

7. The morning after a wild night on the town, I wake up:

a. with my pjs on, alone in my own bed.

b. with a massive hangover.

c. with a massively well-hung man.

8. Boys:

a. lie.

b. Can't live with them, can't live without them.

c. need to take a number if they want to get into my bedroom.

9. The song title that best describes my social life is:

a. "Let's Get Drunk and Screw," Jimmy Buffett

b. "Girls Just Wanna Have Fun," Cyndi Lauper

c. "All By Myself," Celine Dion

10. True or False: Happy hour.

11. Complete the following analogy: Me : Monogamy

  a. J.Lo : Marriage

  b. Britney Spears : Virginity

ANSWER KEY:

1. A: 2; B: 1; C: 3   7. A: 1; B: 2; C: 3

2. A: 1; B: 2; C: 3   8. A: 1; B: 2; C: 3

3. A: 1; B: 2; C: 3   9. A: 3; B: 2; C: 1

4. True: 3; false: 1   10. True: 3; false: 1

5. A: 2; B: 1; C: 3   11. A:1; B: 3

6. True: 3; false: 1

IF YOU SCORED:

11 to 15   Bootyphobic: *The Once-in-a-Blue-Moon Hookup Artist*

You do hook up—as often as February has twenty-nine days or solar eclipses darken the midday sky. In order to irrigate your romantic desert, you need to break your standing date with the remote control and live a little! You're young, you're single, and you're fabulous. A little make-out session here and there never hurt anyone.

16 to 25   Bootylicious: *The Healthy Hookup*

You are a healthy, normal girl. You kick back, relax, have fun, and every once in a while, hook up. Don't change a thing. You'll do fine.

26 to 33   Bootymonster: *The Hookup-a-holic*

Stop in the name of love . . . and STDs . . . and liver damage. We could go on and on, but we are writing this under a deadline. You are a science project gone crazy—a hormone-driven, alcohol-fueled queen of random sexual encounters. Part of us wants you to stop, but the other part wants you to keep doing what you're doing. Obviously, you have a lot of friends who are enjoying the free entertainment you provide. And who are we to deprive them of that?

PART I
THE BARE ESSENTIALS
Setting the Hookup Scene

IN MY OPINION
Real Girls and Guys Define What Hooking Up Means to Them

Everyone talks about hooking up, but no one seems to agree on a single definition. Is it making out? Is it sex? Is it something entirely different? Being the curious people that we are (okay, we're just nosy), we wanted to find out what average guys and girls thought about this vague phrase. We asked them to explain what it means to "hook up." Here's the news from the trenches.

THE RULEMAKERS
Stick to the Guidelines

The Rulemakers play by the book. They think of hooking up in the same way one might think of a competitive sport: with very specific rules and regulations that must be followed in order to constitute legal play. Anything that breaks these rules is simply an illegal use of the hands.

ADAM, 22 To achieve hookup status the following must occur: (1) A man must be able to get the female to a designated area, such as an apartment, house, office, supply closet, airplane bathroom, alley, subway, car, Oval Office, or any other such place where conduct of a sexual nature can be enacted. (2) Both parties must voluntarily remove their clothing, or have the other remove it for them with permission. (3) The man must ejaculate, whether induced by his own hands or by her hands, mouth, vagina, breasts, ears, toes, etc. If any of these three elements is missing, a man has not hooked up.

Some nonhookup activities include:

○ Kissing on the dance floor

○ Sleeping in the same bed with a female

○ Watching porn together

ANDY, 26 Hooking up would be any sexual or sensual act beyond kissing on the lips. This would include a long slow tongue-locking kiss, but would exclude a back rub or shoulder massage. I think this definition is pretty standard, although some friends would include regular kissing on the lips (no tongue), while I would not.

THE BOOB ENTHUSIASTS
Second Base Is the Place

The Boob Enthusiasts feel that breasts are the . . . um . . . stepping stones to a hookup.

ELISA, 25 Hooking up is when you spend a significant amount of time kissing, with at least some action around the upper private parts of the female.

BRANDON, 24 I stand firm that if your hand doesn't at least touch a naked booby, then you didn't hook up. You were just that drunk asshole in the bar trying to get some.

THE PRIVATE EYES
Getting a Room Isn't Just Polite, It's a Necessity

The Private Eyes believe that in order to be a true hookup, the booty must take place behind closed doors. We applaud them for their discretion.

JACLYN, 22 My definition of hooking up is anything more than a kiss and should usually be done behind closed doors, or if done in public, people would yell, "Get a room!"

RACHEL, 26 If he's back at your apartment or you're back at his, it's hooking up.

do not disturb

THE NOT IN DA CLUBBERS
Smooching on the Dance Floor
Doesn't Count

The Not in Da Clubbers maintain that groping and sucking face at a bar or any other type of nightclub establishment is not a hookup. However, you may find them in da club sippin' bub, mama.

JOSH, 24 Hooking up is definitely based on the privacy of the activities. I think that once the two parties enter a private room (or at least create the illusion of privacy) and get intimate (a tongue kiss plus) then it is officially a hookup. Kissing on a dance floor in a bar doesn't count.

DAVID, 27 Hooking up is a minimum of making out and it definitely has to be back at someone's place. Making out in a club doesn't count.

THE LINGUISTS
It's All About the Wording

The Linguists love word play. To them, the term "hooking up" serves as a great way to gloss over or exaggerate what happens between two people when they're feelin' randy.

SHARLENE, 22 Hooking up is defined on a case-by-case basis. Usually when I say I "hooked up with this guy" I just mean "made out." However, if my friends say, "I hooked up with this guy," the next question from me is, "Did you hook up with him or hook up–hook up with him?" The hyphenation of the word implies sex, of course. The next question, depending on your interrogation abilities, is to feel out your friend's definition of sex, which would then help define the hyphenated hookup.

MIKE, 26 I don't consider sex hooking up. I consider hooking up a synonym for making out, but it can also mean more than that. For instance, if two people were "frenching," I would say, "They hooked up a little." If they were frenching, and then he stuck his dick in her face, I would still say that they hooked up. So my range of hooking up can mean many things. But if they had sex, I would not say they just hooked up—sex is different in my mind.

THE EVERYTHING BUTS
There's No S-E-X in Hooking Up

The Everything Buts draw a line between hooking up and hitting a home run.

> **JOLENE, 27** Well, I'm a prude, so I think of just making out as hooking up. Sex is "doing it."

> **PEPPER, 25** A hookup is anything but sex. I never say "I hooked up with him" if we had sex. It's usually "We just hooked up, nothing big happened."

THE KEEPING IT CASUALS
No Couples Allowed

The Keeping It Casuals reiterate the fact that hooking up can't happen between two people who are in a relationship together. So, lucky for most of us, we don't ever have to think about our parents hooking up. Ewww.

JENNIFER, 25 My definition of hooking up is any sexual activity—from kissing to "all the way"—with someone you have no formal relationship with. For example, if you make out with a guy on the first date, it is hooking up; if it is after a year of being together, it is not.

KRISTEN, 24 Hookups occur between complete strangers, acquaintances, or good friends. They are usually unplanned and you can't consider the event a "hookup" if you're in a relationship with the other person or if you already started dating.

Q&A SESSION
Hookup Woes

Still confused about hooking up? Well, maybe we can clarify. Here are some questions and answers about these casual encounters. Hopefully this section will help you figure out what the hell you did last night.

Q: *I made out with this guy on a few separate occasions. All we did was kiss (yes, there was tongue). Is this still considered hooking up?*

A: Whew. We're so relieved there was tongue. Well, it really depends on where the two of you were located during the time of the tonsil hockey incidents. Were you in a crowded place, such as a dark corner of a bar, a booth at Denny's, or the frozen food aisle at the grocery store? If so, you probably did not hook up. Hooking up takes place in a "private" locale, such as your apartment, his dorm room, or a bathroom stall at the bus station.

Q: I got together with this guy at a bar—and things got a little hotter and heavier than first base. (I don't think anyone saw us.) Did we hook up?

A: Yikes. We guarantee that EVERYONE saw you—and pointed in shock, horror, and disgust as you pawed at each other like mating baboons. While privacy remains a main ingredient to a hookup, one can make the argument that doing anything more than making out in front of an audience is also a hookup. We hope you take our advice and get a room next time.

Q: I got drunk one night and slept with my ex-boyfriend. Was this a hookup?

A: Yes, it was a hookup. The general consensus is that hookups only occur between people who are not in a relationship together. And judging by the use of the words "ex" and "slept with" in the same sentence, you probably suffered from another common hookup ailment: short-term memory loss.

Q: How many hookups does it take before I can say that we are "dating"?

A: Unfortunately, the number of times you hook up does not determine your couple status. It's much more complicated than that. If you really want to know where you and your hookup stand, try this formula: Add together the number of estimated DLA (daylight activities) you two have had during the past two weeks with the number of SPC (sober phone conversations). Then, take that number and subtract the number of PBHU (post-bar hookups) and DBC (drunken booty calls). Multiply that by the number of your friends who refrain from rolling their eyes when you talk about him. If you are able to calculate a total using this formula, you are definitely not dating him because you have way too much free time.

Q: Is it still considered a hookup if no one else knows about it?

A: Ah, the beloved Snuffleupagus (see page 164 for more details). We shall answer your question with another question: If a tree falls in the forest and no one hears it, does it still make a sound?

TALK THIS WAY
Impress Your Friends with This Hookup Lingo

Sure, sure. You've heard of the "walk of shame." But do you know what "booty disparity" means? Didn't think so. If you're gonna walk the walk (of shame), you gotta talk the talk. Read on to learn the lingo.

BEER GOOGLE (*verb*): Drunkenly typing the name of the guy you're hooking up with (or would like to hook up with) into every Web search engine in the hopes that you will discover some deep, dark secrets about him. (*"I beer googled him last night, but the only thing I could find was that he finished third in the 100-meter dash at the 1999 Catholic High School League Invitational."*)

BLANK BOY (*noun*): When you identify your hookup by something other than his real name. This could be anything from a distinguishing physical characteristic to the place that you met him. (*"Do you think we'll bump into Bad Hair Boy tonight?"*)

BOOTY DISPARITY (*noun*): The difference between what you think a hookup meant and what he thinks it meant. (*"After Saturday night I had visions of us picking out china together, but then he never called me. Guess we had a bit of a booty disparity."*)

CYBERTEASE (*noun, verb*): When you exchange really flirty suggestive e-mails but the actual hookup doesn't live up to its virtual counterpart. (*"It was a classic case of cyberteasing: His e-mails were so hot they had me clicking my mouse all day long, but when we actually hooked up it was less than stellar."*)

DEFENSIVE DRINKING (verb): How you justify your actions the next day; giving yourself a protective buzz in order to withstand a painful social event. (*"I had to defensive drink my way through Heather's wedding, otherwise I would've never made out with her second cousin in the coat room."*)

DRAPPS (noun): When your hookup suggests that you grab drinks and appetizers; a thinly veiled excuse for a real date. (*"When Jon invited me to Giorgio's last week, I was excited—until he only ordered drapps. I should've known that no one really eats dinner at midnight."*)

DRUNK ENVY (noun): Wishing you had been intoxicated when you hooked up with him, so you could use your clouded judgment and lowered inhibitions as an excuse. Note: If you don't practice defensive drinking you'll most definitely experience drunk envy. (*"I'm having such drunk envy. At least you can say you were wasted when you made out with that guy. I was practically sober when I went home with the dude who looked like Screech."*)

FALSE ADVERTISING (noun): When you think a boy is really hot until you see him without his baseball hat, tan, or guitar. Often applies to athletes, frat boys, lifeguards, and rock stars. (*"He looked hot until he took off his Red Sox cap and I saw his receding hairline—major false advertising."*)

HOMOGENIZED HOOKUP (noun): When you hook up with more than one guy in a group of friends and they all walk, talk, and hook up the exact same way. (*"When Mike and I went home together, I thought I was experiencing déjà vu, but then I realized that I was having a homogenized hookup—he pulls the same moves and says the same lines that his best friend Jason does."*)

HOT POTATO (noun): A guy with whom one or more of your friends has hooked up. (*"Oh, Chris is just a hot potato—me, Jill, and Sarah have all hooked up with him."*)

IMAGINARY FRIENDS (noun): That awkward period of time right after you hook up with a close bud and are both trying to convince yourselves that things are back to normal. (*"I was wondering why he was being so nice, but then it dawned on me that we're playing imaginary friends and he's still totally freaked out by the fact that we hooked up."*)

LAPPED (verb): When an old hookup passes by you in the bar and completely catches you off guard. (*"I was just trying to get the bartender's attention when out of nowhere—WHOOSH—I got lapped by Bad Hair Boy and he left me in his dust."*)

LORD OF THE RING (noun): The phone god who makes the boy you gave your number to at the bar on Saturday night call you by Tuesday. (*"I can't leave my apartment until at least Wednesday because I'm convinced that the Lord of the Ring will work his magic."*)

MUTE (noun): That awkward pause after someone (other than a close friend) asks, "Are you seeing anyone?" What are you supposed to say? I am, but only on Saturday nights, from 2 A.M. to 6 A.M.? (*"I pulled a mute at the dinner table the other night when my mom asked about my romantic life."*)

PG-RATED HOOKUP (noun): Usually describes a hookup in which you just make out and the majority of your clothing stays on. (*"It was a totally PG hookup—I mean, he didn't even get to second base."*)

PRIMPING IN VAIN (verb): Spending hours agonizing over what you're going to wear, blowing out your hair, and blending together three shades of lip gloss to achieve the perfect "natural" hue, only to find out that he's not going out that night. Ironically, you bump into him at the supermarket the next day while you're wearing no makeup and a velour sweatsuit. (*"I was convinced that he was going to be at the bar, but when he didn't show up I was pissed that I wasted an entire afternoon primping in vain."*)

PUZZLING (noun): When you meet up with your friends the next day and collectively piece together what happened the night before. (*"We met for brunch and puzzling, which is how I found out that I made out with Dan in front of everyone."*)

RAINMAN MOMENT (noun): When you consume way too many drinks and your brain goes into a catatonic state in which you become obsessed with one particular idea and won't shut up about it for the rest of the night. (*"After we walked by that great Italian place on the way to the after party, I experienced a Rainman moment and annoyed the hell out of my friends until they took me back to get a slice."*)

REFUELING (verb): When you're not nearly intoxicated enough to see your hookup, so you order one more drink. (*"He's going to be here any second and I'm still totally coherent. Order some tequila shots so we can start refueling pronto."*)

SAFE SEX (noun): Sleeping with an ex-boyfriend. (*"I'm just having safe sex with Josh until Mr. Right comes along."*)

SELECTIVE STORYTELLING (noun): When you spin the previous night's escapades to sound way better than they actually were. (*"I couldn't possibly tell my friends that he fell asleep while going down on me, so I did some selective storytelling and left that part out."*)

SCHICK-BLOCKED (adjective): Opting not to hook up because, well, you've been a little lax with the hair removal lately. ("*I was dying to go home with him, but since I haven't shaved in over a week, I was totally Schick-blocked.*")

STEALTH-BOMB (verb): Hooking up with someone and not noticing how drunk he was until he tells you the next morning. ("*He stealth-bombed me when he said that he almost puked from taking so many shots last night. I mean, I never even saw him with a drink.*")

SUNBURN (noun): That regret you feel immediately after the light of day starts shining through his bedroom windows. ("*The minute I woke up and saw Bad Hair Boy next to me, I felt some severe sunburn.*")

TEAM PLAYER (noun): When you are forced to entertain and (maybe even hook up with) your best friend's hookup's dorky wingman. ("*Stacy forced me to be a team player when her new man's friend came out with us, even though he was 5'3" and a dental hygienist.*")

THE DESPERATE HOUR (noun): The time between 1:30 A.M. and 2:30 A.M. when everyone's frantically searching for their Saturday night soul mate. Often categorized by lots of drunk dialing and rapidly falling standards. ("*He was the only remotely cute guy I could find at the Desperate Hour.*")

TOUR GUIDE (noun): When you hook up with someone's out-of-town guest. (*"I played tour guide with my roommate's friend from high school last weekend."*)

WORK UNDERLOAD (noun): The truth behind his lame excuse that he's too busy with his career to have a real relationship—when you know that all he does at work is sit on his ass in a cubicle, edit his Friendster profile, and surf around on AnnaKournikova.com. (*"He said he's been swamped with a huge project, but I'm pretty sure it's more like work underload since he temps for a living."*)

WHERE THE BOYS ARE
The Hookup Hot Spots

While bars and parties provide the raw ingredients for a hookup (serving up the basics like music, booze, and boys), you still have to put forth some effort to get the ball rolling. Who has time for that? Luckily for you, we live in a society where convenience is cherished, so we have detailed some hot spots that make hooking up as easy and breezy as popping a Lean Cuisine in the microwave: All you have to do is add a little heat and you're good to go.

INVITE-ONLY FUNCTIONS

THE LOWDOWN: Any soiree that requires an RSVP and a new pair of shoes and has an open bar is ideal for hooking up (think engagement party or wedding). Inevitably, you'll end up doing the Electric Slide next to a hottie, with whom you will spend the rest of the evening drinking, dancing, and schmoozing. And because love is already in the air, you might as well raise your glass and toast to the happy couple *and* your happy hookup.

WHO YOU'LL MEET: A distant cousin who your mom swears isn't blood-related

HOT ACCESSORY: A seating card that puts you at the singles table

DRINK: Champagne

PICKUP LINE: "Are you friends with the bride or the groom?"

MUSIC: KC and the Sunshine Band, Lionel Ritchie, and Gloria Estefan

GREEK GET-TOGETHERS

THE LOWDOWN: At a fraternity function it's practically mandatory that you at least get to second base with some guy who considers Abercrombie high fashion. All the ingredients of a hookup are at your disposal: an endless supply of alcohol, ridiculously loud hip-hop music, and lots of empty bedrooms. While you've seen enough after-school specials to know what goes on at the frat house, you just can't help falling under the spell of a "brother" who offers you a Jell-O shot and tells you it's so nice to talk to a girl who's as smart as she is beautiful. Just remember, the Greek letters on the front door really spell S-E-X.

WHO YOU'LL MEET: A cute boy in a backwards hat and a wool sweater with a stripe across the chest

HOT ACCESSORY: A Solo cup

DRINK: Bud Light from a keg

PICKUP LINE: "Wanna check out my room?"

MUSIC: P. Diddy, Big Poppa, and Jay-Z

OFFICE HOLIDAY GATHERINGS

THE LOWDOWN: Company holiday parties or dinners are a breeding ground for the infamous office romance. Maybe it's because it's the first time your coworkers are seeing you in a little black dress and not a sweater set. Or maybe it's because after a few cocktails you start to relax around your officemates, which leads to a bitch-fest about upper management and your measly salaries. Before you know it, you're telling Jon in accounting about your asshole ex-boyfriend and he seems really nice and you never realized how green his eyes were and well . . . no one will ever know if you go home together just this one time . . . right?

WHO YOU'LL MEET: You don't really meet anyone new—you just get to see a very different (meaning drunk) side of everyone from the office.

HOT ACCESSORY: Shrimp cocktail

DRINK: Top-shelf alcohol on the company dollar from 7 to 9 P.M.

PICKUP LINE: "Maybe we should 'bump into each other' under the mistletoe."

MUSIC: Destiny's Child's *8 Days of Christmas* and any Top 40 hit from the past three decades

ANY DISASTER THAT SENDS THE PUBLIC INTO A FRENZY

THE LOWDOWN: Any kind of imminent doom or disaster (think blackouts, blizzards, and floods) can give two people the false notion that it is their very last chance to get it on. But keep this in mind: After the dust settled, no one remembers Y2K, but you'll always be the girl who hooked up with the first guy she could reach on her cell phone simply because she was too scared to die alone.

WHO YOU'LL MEET: Usually this kind of situation sends you straight back into the arms of an ex-boyfriend.

HOT ACCESSORY: A flashlight

DRINK: Water—it's important to stay hydrated.

PICKUP LINE: "I just want to hold you."

MUSIC: AM radio, REM's "It's the End of the World as We Know It (and I Feel Fine)," and the Doors, "The End"

GRADUATION/
EDUCATIONAL MILESTONES

THE LOWDOWN: An event where your grandmother is willing to stick ten dollars in a card that says "Congratulations" is ripe with hookup potential. That's because a "happy ending" (such as graduation) means that you and everyone around you have come to the end of a journey and are about to move forward on different life paths. But instead of wasting your very last night as a college student getting drunk and reminiscing with your sorority sisters (who you never really liked in the first place), why not take this major life moment as an opportunity to finally get it on with someone you've been sweating since freshman year?

WHO YOU'LL MEET: That hot guy from Psych 101

HOT ACCESSORY: Your underage sister (who you have to "pass back" your license to in order to get her into the bar)

DRINK: Celebratory shots

PICKUP LINE: "Didn't you sit behind me in freshman psych?"

MUSIC: Dave Matthews Band, Sarah McLachlan, and Billy Joel

FRESHMAN YEAR OF COLLEGE

THE LOWDOWN: After spending eighteen years living under the same roof as your doting parents and demented big brother, your first year of college equals absolute freedom. As soon as you unpack your yaffa blocks and shower caddy, it truly hits you: "Coeducational" means living with lots of hot guys. Throw together dozens of other college newbies with high expectations and low alcohol tolerances, and you have a recipe for endless hookups. This is the only time in your life when the walk of shame extends the length of a hallway.

WHO YOU'LL MEET: Chris, who hails from Michigan, wears a fleece vest, sports a goatee, and has a black light poster in his room. And oh yeah—did he mention that he's so into Phish?

HOT ACCESSORY: A mini-fridge or a four-foot bong

DRINK: The cheapest case of beer you can find

PICKUP LINE: "What floor do you live on?"

MUSIC: Pink Floyd, Miles Davis, and imported house music

THEME PARTIES

THE LOWDOWN: Ah, it wouldn't be a party without pimps and hoes, togas, or the quintessential Catholic schoolgirls. The theme bash merely serves as an excuse to behave badly and show as much T and A as humanly possible, while still keeping in the spirit of the evening (think "slutty librarian" or "naughty nurse"). Okay, so you probably won't get into a philosophical discussion at "Dress Like a Porn Star Night," but you can definitely connect with your own Ron Jeremy.

WHO YOU'LL MEET: A guy who is using the party theme as an excuse to wear a wife beater and a fake mustache

HOT ACCESSORY: Anything tight, cheap, and vinyl

DRINK: Mystery punch with fruit floating in it

PICKUP LINE: "What are you supposed to be, other than hot?"

MUSIC: Michael Jackson's *Thriller*, *Pure Disco*, *Now That's What I Call Music Volume 15*

SPRINGTIME IN A COLD CLIMATE

THE LOWDOWN: For those of you who live in a place where the sun shines year round, screw you. The rest of us have to suffer through months of gray skies, arctic blasts of wind, and subzero temperatures. But as soon as the ice melts and the flowers bloom, mating season begins. You shed your Nanook of the North look for a tank top and sandals and feel giddy at the sight of so many cute guys in T-shirts. Forget beer goggles—everyone looks better when spring has sprung.

WHO YOU'LL MEET: The guy sitting next to you (wearing flip-flops) at the only bar in your neighborhood that has a patio

WHAT YOU'LL BE WEARING: Way too little, considering it's only fifty-five degrees outside

HOT ACCESSORY: Sunglasses

DRINK: Pitchers of sangria

PICKUP LINE: "Isn't this weather awesome?"

MUSIC: Outkast, Sublime, and the Grateful Dead

DESTINATION GETAWAYS

THE LOWDOWN: A tropical trip provides a new opportunity to rendezvous with someone you would never have the chance to meet in your regular life. Because you have a limited amount of time together, you meet up and make out practically every night. As a result, the whole encounter seems much more romantic and intense than it actually was. The bottom line: By the time you get your pictures developed, Mr. Snorkeling Instructor has long forgotten the night you two cuddled on the beach and he told you that the brightest star in the sky would forever remind him of your smile. (Barf!)

WHO YOU'LL MEET: A devastatingly handsome local with a perfect golden tan

HOT ACCESSORY: Suntan lotion (SPF 4)

DRINK: Margaritas

PICKUP LINE: "I can show you the stuff they don't print in brochures."[3]

MUSIC: Bob Marley, Jimmy Cliff, and UB40

---

[3] Hint: He's talking about his penis.

ADVANCED DEGREES

THE LOWDOWN: Med school, law school, and any other form of postcollegiate education where you can earn yourself some kind of fancy letters after your name provides an ideal environment for hooking up. Unlike undergrad, when you could slide by taking Rocks for Jocks and Intro to Golf, in grad school you actually have to pay attention in class all day and study really hard all night. So on those few precious evenings that you can go out, you and your classmates inevitably end up getting ridiculously wasted and hooking up. FYI: Everybody knows that a study session is just grad-student-speak for "Let's get it on."

WHO YOU'LL MEET: A nerdy, Ivy League grad who doesn't want anything to get between him and his chosen career path

HOT ACCESSORY: A laptop

DRINK: Red Bull, which will help keep you awake while you're studying

PICKUP LINE: "Your answer in Constitutional Law was riveting."

MUSIC: The sound of silence . . . you're "studying," remember?

DOMESTIC BLISS
The Hookup-Friendly Bachelorette Pad

S o you've got the guy and he says, "Let's go back to your place." Here's how to make sure that your apartment is a hookup haven, rather than a hookup deterrent.*

---

* For starters, guys are always freaked out by those creepy Anne Geddes baby-in-a-peapod, baby-in-a-flowerpot, and baby-in-a-pumpkin-patch pictures.

	PROUDLY DISPLAY	STASH AWAY	BURN IMMEDIATELY
Wall Decor	Framed photo of you, circa last year, looking fab	Framed photo of you, circa freshman year, looking fat	Framed photo of your cat, circa last Halloween (looking quite handsome in the tux you dressed him up in)
Food/Drink	A bottle of wine and a bowl of strawberries	A bottle of Bud and pizza left over from last weekend	A forty-ounce bottle of malt liquor and your stash of Ramen noodles
DVDs	*Goodfellas, Cruel Intentions, The Sopranos: Season Three, The Simpsons*	*Save the Last Dance, Clueless, Girls Just Wanna Have Fun*	*The Runaway Bride, You've Got Mail, Bounce, Faces of Death 1 through 6*
Music	Miles Davis, Outkast, Led Zeppelin	Alanis Morissette, John Mayer, Sarah McLachlan	Barbra Streisand, Indigo Girls, Slayer

	PROUDLY DISPLAY	STASH AWAY	BURN IMMEDIATELY
Books	Anything in *The Onion* series, *The Kama Sutra, Fear and Loathing in Las Vegas*	*Chicken Soup for the Soul, The South Beach Diet, Sweet Valley High* books (don't deny it—you still have them)	*Depression for Dummies, The Rules,* anything with Fabio painted on the cover
Bathroom Finds	Listerine, antibacterial hand soap, reading material	Proactiv, pantyliners, economy-sized jar of Vaseline	Summer's Eve, EPT, Jolene Facial Hair Bleach
Athletic Equipment	A yoga mat (to show how flexible you are)	Your ab roller	Richard Simmons's *Sweatin' to the Oldies*
Clothes	Jeans, a pair of killer heels, a lacy black bra	Velour sweatsuit, UGG boots, granny panties	Control-top tights, "footie" PJs, your period undies
Bedding	Freshly washed sheets	Flannel sheets	"Mr. Blankie"

YOUR OWN PERSONAL
HOOKUP CONTRACT
Break This and There Will Be Hell to Pay

Do you need a little incentive to help eliminate hookup-induced drama and trauma from your life? Well, have no fear—fill out the following hookup contract (which is oh-so-legally binding), cut it out, and hang it on your fridge next to your magnetic poetry and gas/electric bill. There it will forever serve as a reminder that you should leave the major dramatic performances to someone like Tori Spelling in the Lifetime movie classic *Mother, May I Sleep with Danger?* (You couldn't top that no matter how hard you tried, so do yourself a favor and leave the tears up to the professionals.)

MY HOOKUP CONTRACT

On [INSERT TODAY'S DATE], I, [INSERT MY NAME] willfully enter into this contract with myself, to ensure that any hookup from this day forward will remain free of unnecessary drama (meaning the kind that makes a guy refer to me as "the psycho"). In particular, I vow that I will never, under any circumstances*, commit the following offenses:

1. I will refrain from wearing a mini and stilettos AND a tube top to the bar—especially in the dead of winter—in a misguided attempt to find my Prince Charming. I will realize that these types of "ensembles" are best reserved for Halloween or theme parties (see "Where the Boys Are" on page 46 for more details).

2. I will resist the urge to mentally combine my first name with a hookup's last name "just to see how it sounds." In fact, I will get that out of my system right now and then delete it from my memory forever: [INSERT MY FIRST NAME] [INSERT HIS LAST NAME].

---

* "Circumstances" refers to any events including, but not limited to: the consumption of multiple cocktails in a short period of time, a sighting of an ex-boyfriend with a new girlfriend, a desire to make the aforementioned ex-boyfriend jealous, acute boredom, my birthday, or a full moon.

3. I will not steal a friend's hookup, no matter how wrong he is for her or how right he is for me.

4. I will NEVER be *that girl*, and by *that girl* I mean the one who runs out of a bar with mascara dripping down her cheeks, sobbing on her cell phone, "I can't believe that asshole had the nerve to talk to someone else right in front of me! Did he really think that I wasn't going to get pissed? Who does he think he is? Do you think he's going to call me later?"

5. I will not drunkenly dial him. In the event that I have had too much to drink and begin frantically scrolling through my phone's address book, I will relinquish custody of my mobile phone to [INSERT NAME OF MOST TRUSTWORTHY FRIEND]. Once the temporary guardian has control of my cell, she will determine when I am fit to make sound dialing judgments. (This same rule applies for pagers, Blackberrys, or any other portable electronic devices that have the ability to instantaneously transmit embarrassing messages. Unfortunately, I am on my own regarding e-mail and IM.)

6. I will not feel guilty about staying in on a Saturday night and watching *Golden Girls* reruns in my sweatpants. I will realize that there are plenty of other weekends to go out and hit the town, but how often do they show the episode where Blanche finds out that her brother is gay?

7. I will not define myself by how often I hook up. I will remember that quality over quantity is a good thing. (For example, I'd rather have one pair of jeans that makes my ass look ridiculously hot, as opposed to a whole closet full of mediocre denim.)

8. I will not wait in obsessive agony for him to call me. Instead, I will give myself permission to call him. However, I must not do so in a passive-aggressive manner that will put the ball back in his court (i.e., leaving a message on his cell phone while he is at work, dialing his work extension during the weekend, or calling his apartment line while he is away on vacation). I will come to terms with the fact that this is a vicious cycle that always concludes in the same manner: with me waiting for the fucking phone to fucking ring.

9. I will not assume that I'm in a room full of voyeurs who have any interest in watching me and some guy I just met engage in explicit PDA. That's just icky.

10. I will not take anything too seriously. Rather, I will arm myself with a wicked sense of humor.

Any breach of this contract will result in stiff penalties, including some or all of the following: (1) Making myself watch C-SPAN instead of *E! News Live* every night for a week; (2) Staying in and making it a Blockbuster night with the following movies: *Waterworld*, *Yentl*, and *My Dog Skip*; (3) Trading in my pilates tape for Richard Simmons's *Sweatin' to the Oldies*; (4) Dressing up for Halloween as a bunny, and no, I don't mean a half-naked Playboy bunny, but a mall-style Easter bunny with whiskers and a basket; (5) Getting up onstage at karaoke night and belting out the Divinyls' "I Touch Myself"—completely sober.

Signed

_____

Dated

_____

PART II

TYPECASTING
The Players
in the Game

HOOKUP
So Much More Than a Verb

As most of you know, "hook up/hookup" is quite a versatile word. Not only is it a verb ("*Can you believe I hooked up with him?*"), it is also a noun that has two meanings. First of all, it refers to the person with whom you are hooking up ("*I only call my hookup after 1 A.M.*"). Secondly, it denotes the actual nonrelationship ("*That was the worst hookup ever.*"). And not all hookups are exactly the same. Much like dogs, there are several different breeds of hookup, each having its own distinct traits and dispositions. While a girl may encounter all types of hookups, after careful observation and research we've narrowed the playing field down to fourteen of the most common ones. Do any of these look familiar to you?

THE ARE-YOU-MY-BOYFRIEND?
The Nonrelationship Relationship

THE SCENARIO: After a few weeks of hooking up regularly, you feel a boyfriend breakthrough coming on (he's finally waking up and realizing how dinner- and daylight-worthy you are). You have visions of coupledom dancing in your head, in which you spend evenings snuggling on the couch, watching reruns, and complaining about your girlfriends, who are still scrounging around the bars for random boys to hook up with. (Seriously, why can't they just find a great guy and settle down like you have?)

HIM, IN A NUTSHELL: Your costar in the Are-You-My-Boyfriend? drama is a slightly better-than-average guy who seems like a great idea at the time. He's semi-smart, semi-successful, semi-good-looking, semi-your-type, but not *completely* any one of these things. For some reason—maybe you're getting over a boyfriend, maybe you two click as friends, or maybe you're confused by the regularity of your hookups—you believe that this lukewarm prospect is really a red-hot commodity. Blinded by circumstances, you wish him into the perfect boyfriend.

While the Are-You-My-Boyfriend? boy comes in all shapes, styles, and scents, chances are, he can be described by one or more of the following: He is the Gap of guys. This means that he is universally appealing to all girls, safe, and not too flashy. If he were a color, he'd be khaki. Maybe he belonged (or belongs) to a fraternity. He has a healthy appetite for blondes, boobs, and full-contact sports. Upon meeting him, your mother would approve. After you guys stop hooking up (because you can never actually break up), you will realize that he was completely unremarkable.

THE UPSIDE: Having an Are-You-My-Boyfriend? is like eating an entire pint of Häagen-Dazs Café Mocha Frappe without having to worry about the calories. Basically, you get a "boyfriend" without having to deal with being a "girlfriend."

EXAMPLE: Him: "Babe, will you scratch my back?"

You: "Um, no."

BUYER BEWARE: This is the David Copperfield of hookups: It looks, feels, and sounds like a relationship, but it could very well be one clever, stunning illusion.

> **EXAMPLE:** His friends act surprised when they see you two together.

IDENTIFYING FEATURES OF THE ARE-YOU-MY-BOYFRIEND? HOOKUP

1. **THE MIDDAY BOOTY CALL:** Normally you'd get a call between the designated "hookup hours" of 1 A.M. and 3 A.M., but with an are-you-my-boyfriend? hookup, he sends you an e-mail at work around 4 P.M. that says, "hey, u around tonite?" You then forward it to your three best friends to analyze. The long-awaited verdict: He wants to hang out with you tonight. After discussing with your gay coworker, you e-mail him back approximately six hundred words describing how your week's been so far, how your day is going, what you had for lunch, and oh yeah, that you just happen to be around tonight.

2. **MORNING-AFTER BRUNCH:** It's likely that after a night of nookie, your Are-You-My-Boyfriend? will suggest grabbing something to eat. So the two of you sit in a booth at some

shitty diner and you pretend to be super-svelte by ordering an egg-white omelette with dry wheat toast while you're secretly drooling over his bacon and home fries. You make idle chitchat about your siblings, future vacation plans, and the ever-safe childhood pets. If your waiter didn't know better, he'd swear you two were a real-deal couple.

3. **DINNER AND A MOVIE, NO INTOXICATION NECESSARY:** You sometimes go out on dates—real dates that you thought were reserved only for couples who knew each other's middle names. But alas, here you are, fresh from dinner at the local pizza joint, waiting in line for the 10:15 P.M. showing of the latest action-adventure movie (don't hold your breath for a romantic comedy). The catch? He buys the tickets, but you pay for the popcorn, soda, and gummy bears.

4. **NEWFOUND PSYCHIC ABILITIES:** Since you guys started hooking up, you've become quite a mind reader. Because this type of hookup so closely resembles a real relationship, but lacks the "What are we?" talk, you're left making the assumption that he really wants to be your steady gig. You just don't want to ruin this "rclationship" by clueing the guy in on the fact that yes, you two are actually in one.

THE BOYFRIEND	THE ARE-YOU-MY-BOYFRIEND?
Kisses you on the forehead before you go to sleep.	Asks you to give him head before he goes to sleep.
Leaves your place early in the morning to get coffee and bagels before you wake up.	Leaves your place early in the morning.
Throws you a surprise birthday party.	Accidentally shows up at the bar where you're having your birthday party.
Fills your Vicodin prescription when you get your wisdom teeth removed.	Steals your Vicodin prescription when you get your wisdom teeth removed.
Buys you a pearl necklace.	Gives you a pearl necklace.
Washes and returns the T-shirt you left at his place.	Uses the T-shirt you left at his place as a rag after he checks the oil in his car.
Went to Cancun on spring break his freshman year of school.	Going to Cancun on spring break this year . . . and he graduated in 1998.
Offers to help your roommate move her bed.	Offers to help your roommate break in her bed.
Puts on Marvin Gaye for mood music.	Tells you that mood music is "gay."
His friends refer to you as "Jen." Your name is Jennifer.	His friends refer to you as "Jen." Your name is Alison.
Has a framed photo of you on his dresser.	Refuses to have his photo taken with you.

MORNING-AFTER ATTIRE: You are almost always spotted leaving his place in your tightest jeans, three-inch stilettos, and his Greek Week T-shirt, size XXL, circa 1999.

WHY IT ENDS: Remember those really cool "Choose Your Own Adventure" books from the '80s? Well, ending this hookup is just like that. You can either let the guy pull the plug or you can create your own version of a relatively happy ending. In the case of the Are-You-My-Boyfriend? you can choose between:

> **ENDING 1:** He'll have an epiphany that he hasn't hooked up with anyone else in months, which will result in a massive panic attack, which then will result in the dumping of you.
>
> **ENDING 2:** You'll get tired of mouthing the word "boyfriend" when introducing him to your friends and decide that you'd rather be single than fake date him.

WHY YOU'RE BETTER OFF WITHOUT HIM

In case you need motivation to choose Ending 2, here's a handy list of reasons why he sucked, still sucks, and will forever, until the end of time, suck:

1. His only loyalty is to his Fantasy Football team.

2. He calls his friends by their last names and greets them with a secret handshake (often a "knuckle pound").

3. His screen saver features a tasteful photo of Paris Hilton.

4. He still goes to Dave Matthews Band concerts.

5. His mom buys him underwear and socks (and washes them).

6. He makes fun of you for always ordering salad dressing on the side . . . but he refuses to drink anything other than low-carb beer.

7. His idea of dressing up means a bright blue Banana Republic button-down shirt instead of a bright blue Banana Republic T-shirt.

8. He regularly quotes lines from *Braveheart*.

9. He thinks Connecticut would be a nice place to settle down.

10. He says "yo."

THE METROMAN
The Tragically Hip Urban Metrosexual

THE SCENARIO: You lock eyes across the crowded room at the Kenneth Cole sample sale, and you both make a move for the same black leather blazer. You point out that it's a ladies' jacket, but he doesn't back down. He says he'll let you have the coat if you let him take you for a latte. You're so smitten by his expertly tousled hair and laser-bleached smile that you have to say yes. Before long you are hooking up with a Metroman. He's a hip hottie with a great fashion sense, a taste for the cooler things in life, and two major drawbacks: (1) He's too good NOT to be gay.

(2) If he isn't actually gay, there's still one ultra-important man in his life that you could never compete with: himself.

Although you would give anything for the "normal" boys you've hooked up with to have had your Metroman's interest in personal grooming and Pottery Barn, you can't help but wonder, "Am I just another accessory?" or even worse, "Am I just a phase on the way to full-blown homosexuality?"

HIM, IN A NUTSHELL: The Metroman (more commonly known as the "Metrosexual") is a new breed of urban superhero. Able to withstand a back and brow wax without flinching, fresher-smelling than a Sephora store, and comfortable enough with his sexuality to shun any sport that requires a cup, he seems like the perfect guy. He possesses an almost uncanny talent for scoping out the latest fashion trends before they become so yesterday. He owns a DVD collection more extensive than Blockbuster's. He wears nonprescription reading glasses. He lives in a loft. He claims that carbs make him look bloated. He drinks at lounges and dines at fusion restaurants. He exudes hipness, affluence, worldliness, and nuevo-domestication. He is the perfect mix of masculinity and femininity. Essentially, he is the woman you strive to become.

THE UPSIDE: Since the Metroman has such good taste, it's a huge ego boost that he thinks you're hot enough to hook up with.

> **EXAMPLE:** He returned the three-hundred-thread-count Polo sheets his mom bought him because he thought they were itchy.

BUYER BEWARE: While he may have all the vanity and fashion sense of a chick, he lacks the sensitivity of one.

> **EXAMPLE:** When you're hooking up with him, he asks how often you get waxed. You reply, "About once a month," to which he snorts, "Well. Maybe you should think about making that twice a month."

IDENTIFYING FEATURES OF THE METROMAN HOOKUP

1. **CONTAGIOUS SNOBBERY:** Even though your Metroman doesn't exactly take you to all the fab restaurants and lounges he raves about, that doesn't stop you from becoming a walking, talking Zagat Survey. As a result, you find yourself asking the waitress at Friendly's if the chicken fingers are free-range.

2. OMD (OBSESSIVE MAINTENANCE DISORDER):

Ever since you met him, your schedule is packed with grooming appointments and workout sessions. You're so busy getting waxed, plucked, highlighted, and manicured in an effort to look hot that your yoga-toned ass is too tired to meet him at the new bar downtown.

3. YOU, THIS SEASON'S HOTTEST ACCESSORY:

Just like he trades in his cell phone for the new model every month, you have a feeling that your time is limited. It's not that he doesn't like you enough to actually date you. It's just that this dude is way too hip to be caught without the latest and greatest life has to offer.

4. THE HE'S-TOO-GAY-TO-NOT-BE-GAY WINGMAN:

It seems like every Metroman has a token friend who is just slightly more feminine and seemingly gay than he is. While the purpose of the wingman is unknown, one popular theory is that the Metroman keeps him around to prove to his super-straight friends that he isn't gay. No matter what his purpose is, this little sidekick makes you feel mighty uncomfortable. You swear that he once turned around and mouthed, "He's mine!" to you while your hookup was paying for his martini at the bar.

IS HE HETERO, METRO, OR GAY?

	HETERO	METRO	GAY
Favorite Drink	Anything in a pint, keg, or can	Sake or a full-bodied Spanish red	A Midori Sour on a full-bodied Spanish pool boy
What's in His CD Player	The Rolling Stones, Jay-Z, Metallica	A healthy mix of genres: Sinatra, The Roots, The Shins	Madonna, Britney, Cher
Footwear	Nikes	Yoji Yamamoto limited-edition Adidas	Gucci loafers—no socks
Must-See TV	*Monday Night Football*	The Food Network	*E! True Hollywood Story*
Electronic Gadget	TiVo	Mac Powerbook	The Epilady
Hair Must-Have	Shampoo	Organic rosemary conditioner	Highlights
Accessory of Choice	Leather wallet	Leather wrist cuff	Leather collar
Dirty Secret	Gets spray-tanned on a weekly basis	Used to be chubby	Once wore white shoes after Labor Day
What He Calls You	Some Girl	My New Girl	Giiiirl!!!!

TYPECASTING

	HETERO	METRO	GAY
How He Greets You	A hug	A quick peck on the lips	Air kisses (both cheeks)
Pet	A Lab named Jerry	A Wheaton named Jerry	A pug named Jerry
Occupation	Investment banker	Graphic designer	A "stylist" of any kind

MORNING-AFTER ATTIRE: Since he refuses to sleep at your place (the sheet thing), you are often spotted leaving his place in his fancy sweatpants and cashmere sweater—neither of which he'll remember lending to you.

WHY IT ENDS: He simply doesn't have time to have a relationship with you. There's room in his life for only one beautiful person.[5]

---

[5] Himself.

METROMEN MAKE GREAT FRIENDS

Just because you and your metro couldn't hack it romantically doesn't mean your relationship can't morph into something way more fulfilling. Here, ten reasons why you should become besties with him:

- You can still kiss your best friend on New Year's Eve—only this year you won't look like a lesbian.

- He'll eventually trust you enough to show you the pictures from the summer when his parents sent him to fat camp.

- You both have a huge crush on Seth from *The O.C.*

- He secretly despises *Monday Night Football*.

- You wear the same size jeans (okay, he's a tiny bit smaller than you are).

- He'll actually invite you to all of the cool restaurants and lounges he's always yapping about.

- He takes salsa lessons with you.

- He gets you on his eyebrow waxing schedule.

- Your friends can entertain themselves making "Is he or isn't he?" bets.

- He loves your mom.

DRINK TILL HE'S CUTE
The Fall-Down-Drunk Hookup

THE SCENARIO: You and your girlfriends meet up at your pad to have some cocktails before hitting the town. One hour and two vodka-with-a-splash-of-tonics later, you arrive at the bar and immediately order a round of shots. A cute boy approaches you and offers to buy you a Cosmo—then a shot of tequila, followed by a Jack and Coke, etc., etc., etc. By now you're feeling really festive so you start making out with your new "friend." To celebrate your budding relationship you—what else—order more shots and go back to making out. When you come up for air, you have a slight anxiety attack and wonder if he's actually as cute as you had originally thought.

So you ask your best friend to tell you *honestly* if he's hot, heinous, or somewhere in between. She says she *honestly* thinks he's great, tells you to go for it, then tosses back a shot and dances into the wall. You trust her impeccable judgment and head to another bar for a few more cocktails with Mr. Great. Five hours later you wake up with the most excruciating headache—and that's definitely not your ceiling.

HIM, IN A NUTSHELL: Painting a picture of your drunken conquest is a lot like compiling a police sketch. A bunch of witnesses, who weren't exactly in the best frame of mind when the "incident" took place, offer up their vague descriptions. Then it's your responsibility to take these random  pieces and complete the puzzle. This is never an easy task because: (1) The bar was dark. (2) You had one too many shots to really remember anything. (3) You drank all those rounds of shots with your friends, who also don't remember anything.

Even after you sit down with your friends and construct what you think is an accurate portrait of the man in question, you were probably a little off the mark. *You and your friends thought:* His name was Jared, he had pretty blue eyes, and he owned his own business. *Reality check:* His name was Darryl, he had a lazy eye, and his hair was business in the front and party in the back.

THE UPSIDE: You're not as reserved as you normally would be upon meeting a guy.

> **EXAMPLE:** Seconds after finding out his name, you give him a lap dance.

BUYER BEWARE: Two very important words: Beer goggles

> **EXAMPLE:** You go home with someone who you think is a dead ringer for Mark Wahlberg in *The Italian Job,* only to wake up with a dude who looks more like Donnie Wahlberg, circa NKOTB.

IDENTIFYING FEATURES OF THE DRINK-TILL-HE'S-CUTE HOOKUP

1. **TRIPLE-X PDA:** Even though you swear that you're so NOT the girl who makes out in bars, once you've had a few drinks in you, you just can't help but start smooching. This would be cute, except for the fact that you are straddling him and your shirt is unbuttoned.

2. **"DEEP" CONVERSATIONS:** As the result of a heavy dose of booze, you convince yourself that you and your new friend are connecting on a profound level. To the sober world, though, your riveting conversation consists of you nodding and slurring "totally" as your guy babbles on and on about hedge funds.

3. **ACID-TRIP-STYLE FLASHBACKS:** You can't remember what you did last night, let alone who in the world you did it with. But then, days later, you might be watching a movie or sitting in a meeting at work and BAM!!—out of nowhere you get a crystal-clear vision of him without a shirt and ewww . . . he had man boobs.

4. THE LONG ROAD TO RECOVERY: Waking up with a killer hangover is bad enough, but waking up with a pounding headache, intense nausea, and a random boy snoring in your ear truly sucks. At this point, you must take one of the two following courses of action: Either kick him out if he's at your place ("*I forgot I had to work today. Sorry. Yeah, we'll do this again sometime . . .*"), or begin the journey back home. No matter what you do, it will take a massive amount of effort before you can down a gallon of water, turn on Comedy Central, and spend the rest of the day ALONE in bed, detoxifying.

MORNING-AFTER ATTIRE: The same outfit you wore to the bar the night before, minus your underwear, which mysteriously disappeared at some point in the evening

HOW DRUNK ARE YOU? THE SCIENCE OF YOUR BUZZ

Since you're a big girl, we don't need to tell you to consume alcohol responsibly (didn't you see *Leaving Las Vegas?*). But for those times that you give your liver a workout, here's a look at what *really* happens as your night (and booze intake) progresses.

BAC (BLOOD ALCOHOL CONCENTRATION)	CLINICAL EFFECTS	WHAT THAT REALLY MEANS YOU'RE DOING
Out-to-Dinner-with-Your-Parents Drunk		
.02–.03 1 drink or less	No visible effects of intoxication at this stage; slight mood elevation	All of your personal belongings are still in order. You can differentiate the cute guys from the not-so-cute ones.
Happy Hour Drunk		
.05–.06 2 drinks	Feeling of mild sedation, relaxation; exaggerated emotion; impaired judgment about continued drinking	You feel like dancing to songs you would normally find really annoying. A friend buys you a shot of Jägermeister (which always makes you puke), and you think, "Why the hell not?" and knock it back.
Can't-Feel-Your-Fingers-or-Toes Drunk		
.07–.09 3 or 4 drinks	Beginnings of hearing and visual impairment; disturbance of balance; increased confidence; loss of coordination	You trip and fall on the dance floor. Your "whisper" sounds like a shout to everyone else.
Is-the-Room-Spinning-or-Is-It-Just-Me? Drunk		
.11–.19 5 or 6 drinks	Major physical and mental impairment; blurred vision and slurred speech; increased pain threshold	When your ex's new girlfriend strolls into the room, you give her a big hug and say, "It's soooo good to see you!" Someone accidentally burns you with a cigarette and you exclaim, "Don't worry, I'm fiiiine."

The Wino-Off-the-Streets Drunk

| .20–.24 | Loss of motor control; disorientation; in need of assistance | You violently shake your booty to 50 Cent and take out innocent bystanders in the process. |
| 7 or 8 drinks | | You can't tell the difference between the bathroom door and the wall. |

Behind-the-Music: Mötley-Crüe **Drunk**

| .25 and up | Coma; unconsciousness; possible death | The only thing you're hooking up with tonight is a stomach pump. |
| You've cleaned out your parents' liquor cabinet | | Go straight to Betty Ford if you ever get this bad. |

WHY IT ENDS: Experts say that it takes your body one hour to process a drink. According to this formula, your love affair will end in five or six hours.

ALL PARTIED OUT

While hitting the town like a wild woman and having a crazy drunken affair always seems like a good idea at the time, here are some signs that you should probably head home—alone—and cuddle with the toilet:

- You take "It's gettin' hot in here, so take off all your clothes" literally.

- You open up a tab . . . at 2 A.M.

- You make six new best friends in the ladies' room.

- You've gone through an entire pack of cigs (and you don't even smoke).

- The guy standing by the pool table (with the lazy eye) starts to look attractive.

- You're doing the running man on the dance floor . . . by yourself.

- You seem to have lost everything you brought to the bar, including your friends.

- You sit down at a table and "rest your eyes" for a minute.

- The DJ puts on "Angel" by Shaggy and you start bawling because the song is just "so sweet."

- Your eye makeup has migrated south, making you look like a cross between Johnny Depp in *Pirates of the Caribbean* and Alice Cooper.

MR. DECEMBER
The Older Man

THE SCENARIO: You tag along with a friend to a fancy housewarming party. As you stand in the kitchen and pick at the veggie platter, a tall, dark, handsome stranger waltzes in and makes a beeline for the Merlot. *Wow,* you think, as you gaze at his salt-and-pepper hair and broad shoulders. *When did dads start looking so hot?* You flag down your friend and press her for more information about this mystery DILF. She laughs and says that while he has definitely lived through more presidencies than you have, there are no wife or kids in his life. You breathe a sigh of relief, think of something grown-up to say,* and stroll on over to this mature stranger. Faster than you can say Catherine Zeta-Jones, you are hooking up with a man who recalls—in vivid detail—all of the events covered in both *I Love the 80s* and *I Love the 70s.*

---

* Like, "How about that federal interest rate?" We don't know what it means, but it sounds good!

HIM, IN A NUTSHELL: Mr. December is way more sophisticated than the sloppy drunk boys you bump into at the local pub. He has a taste for the finer things in life (like aperitifs, cigars, and of course, you). He's charming and chivalrous (at least, in a superficial, opening-doors-for-women type of way), as well as mentally and financially stable. Gone are the days of maxing out credit cards to buy four-foot-tall subwoofers and backpacking through Europe in search of life's big answers and places where he can legally smoke hashish. Mr. December feels confident enough to take everything in stride.

Suddenly, guys your age seem like Pabst Blue Ribbon in a can next to this dark, rich snifter of Rémy Martin. Sure, he may have headed off to college while you were still playing with My Little Ponys, but he's sexy, he's worldly, and he's got a home office. Most guys you know have a home bathroom, a home futon, and a home PlayStation 2.

THE UPSIDE: You feel sophisticated and glamorous just being around him.

> **EXAMPLE:** He makes espresso in the morning and actually drinks it out of those little cups.

TYPECASTING

BUYER BEWARE: Calm your hormones, Ms. Zeta-Jones. Older doesn't necessarily mean wiser, sweeter, or better. This could very well be the spoiled white wine of hookups: You leave it sitting around for months thinking that it will actually get better with age, and when you finally pop open the cork, it ends up tasting like something that came out of a jug.

> **EXAMPLE:** He still reads *Maxim*.

IDENTIFYING FEATURES OF THE MR. DECEMBER HOOKUP

1. **PLAYING CATCH-UP:** He knows more than you do about some things. It's as simple as that. Even if you read Dostoyevsky for fun or compute derivatives in your sleep, his extra years give him certain advantages in the life experience category. Always an overachiever, you find yourself straining for something intelligent to say when he and his friends veer the conversation into "old man territory" and discuss capital gains taxes and "summering." But don't worry—just because you could give two shits about Nantucket doesn't make you any less intelligent than he is.

2. **MATERIAL GIRL:** He buys you nice sparkly things that come in pretty boxes—usually the type of gifts you only  see in magazines or fancy store windows.[7] Before you start thinking of yourself as a high-priced call girl, keep in mind that these tokens of appreciation are relative to his financial status. (Remember when you used to be able to take out twenty dollars from the ATM and survive on it for an entire weekend?)

3. **STONE COLD SOBER:** Often, you wake up in the morning after hooking up with Mr. December and realize that something very important is missing: a hangover. Unlike most nonrelationships, you and your older man don't usually need Jack or the Captain to get the party started. Shockingly enough, maybe he's outgrown getting plowed into oblivion and prefers to drink alcohol for the taste.

---

[7] Do people really wear tennis bracelets while they play tennis?

4. WOLF IN TAILORED CLOTHING: Mr. December comes from a different generation. (Okay, not like he remembers the Civil War or anything, but you know what we mean.) He still believes in chivalry, which can be confusing because it makes this hookup really resemble a relationship. But strip away the manners and expensive cologne and you still have a guy you're just hooking up with.

MORNING-AFTER ATTIRE: You lounge away the A.M. hours in the cashmere slippers and matching robe he bought for you.

WHAT A DIFFERENCE A DECADE (OR TWO) MAKES

	MR. DECEMBER	GUYS YOUR AGE
Interests	Politics, travel, and golf	Sleep, *The Simpsons*, and Lindsay Lohan (okay, her cans)
Primary Social Outlet	Dinner parties	Parties till he pukes

	MR. DECEMBER	GUYS YOUR AGE
Digs	Which one— the penthouse or the lake house?	A basement-level dump, complete with kegerator and Glade plug-in strips
Career Aspirations	Retire at age forty-five	Find a job where he doesn't have to wake up before twelve o'clock
Fashion Inspiration	Mr. Big	Mr. Timberlake
Most Prized Possession	His humidor	His iPod
He Smells Like . . .	Ralph Lauren Polo	Drakkar Noir
Favorite Eighties Memory	Reaganomics	*Thundercats*
Pet	A fifty-gallon aquarium filled with exotic fish	A mongrel named Joey who has an incontinence problem
Fitness Regimen	Meets with personal trainer three times a week in preparation for his first triathlon	Rolls around his neighborhood on a Razor scooter
Underwear	Silk boxers	Goes commando because "the boys just wanna be free"
In Ten Years He Will Be . . .	Dating someone younger than you	Finally drinking beer out of glasses

WHY IT ENDS: You get tired of going to cigar bars and drinking fine wines, and it also dawns on you that he's not older and sophisticated—he's just old.

ADULT ED

Okay, maybe the love affair didn't last, but that doesn't mean you didn't learn something from your Mr. December. Here's some helpful knowledge you took away from hooking up with him:

- It's never too early to start investing in a 401K.

- You learned how to play chess.

- Oysters on the half shell aren't that gross after all.

- You know when to use a 5-iron and when to use a 5-wood.

- You can smell a Cuban cigar a quarter of a mile away.

- 60 Minutes can be quite riveting at times.

- Thanks to him, you now know how to drive his stick shift. (If you laughed at the "stick" part, you are way too immature to be hooking up with an older guy in the first place.)

- Just like with Coke and Pepsi, there really is a difference between Belvedere and Grey Goose. (Who knew?)

- Picking out the perfect cut of meat is a true art form.

- Classical music can be enjoyed everywhere—not just in elevators.

PASS THE SIPPY CUP
The Younger Guy

THE SCENARIO: Your friend begs you to come with her to her younger brother's nineteenth birthday party, and being the trooper that you are, you agree to spend the evening at "The Landing"— a college watering hole that considers a library card an acceptable form of identification. You push your way up to the bar and smirk at a group of barely legal girls, who are wearing napkin-sized tops and throwing back kamikaze shots. Just as the bartender hands you a dirty martini, someone knocks into you and spills the entire glass down your shirt. When you turn around to tell off the drunken klutz who entered you in an impromptu wet T-shirt contest, you come face-to-face with an adorable, baby-faced boy who is holding a wad of napkins. He apologizes profusely and buys you another drink. He asks you what year you are in school and you chuckle and tell him that actually, you're twenty-five and work in advertising. You both start laughing awkwardly and you notice that he's blushing, which makes him look even younger—and cuter. While you realize that the two of you have nothing in common—he goes to keg parties and you go to staff meetings— you just can't help pushing him into the bathroom and showing him what it's like to be seduced by an older woman.

HIM, IN A NUTSHELL: It's not like you're *really* robbing the cradle, since he's only about six years younger than you (which is hardly Mrs. Robinson territory). It's just that there's a huge maturity gap between an "I'm still undecided about my major" college student and an "I'm going to be vice president of my company in five years" twenty-something career girl. For starters, he looks like an Abercrombie ad come to life: He wears a beaded hemp necklace and a trucker hat, and you're almost positive that he doesn't own any footwear other than sneakers.

He lives with three roommates in an apartment that consists of one couch, one dartboard, no toilet paper, and, like, five hundred DVDs. He uses slang terms that you used five years ago, only he throws them into conversation in an ironic, it's-so-out-it's-in way. He considers *Bill and Ted's Excellent Adventure* a classic example of American filmmaking, and he quoted *South Park* in his high school yearbook. He's not relationship material by any means, but you're having a blast rediscovering the joys of getting high and watching *Iron Chef*.

THE UPSIDE: He's so psyched about hooking up with an older chick that he treats you like a goddess.

> **EXAMPLE:** **He drops out of the beer pong tournament at the last minute just so he can hang out with you.**

BUYER BEWARE: He doesn't have a lot of focus or direction.

> **EXAMPLE:** **He can never decide whether he wants to smoke out of his bong or his bowl.**

IDENTIFYING FEATURES OF
THE PASS-THE-SIPPY-CUP HOOKUP

1. **MARATHON SEX:** While the guys your own age are hardly candidates for Viagra, you can't believe how long your boy toy can go for. And what he lacks in experience and skill (a little to the left . . . ummm . . . the other left) he definitely makes up for in stamina and persistence. In fact, he gives you such a workout that you've cut back your cardio sessions.

2. **BINGE DRINKING:** Like any typical college student, he has an endless enthusiasm for drinking, which never shows signs of dissipating. Whether it's guzzling 40s with his friends in the afternoon, doing keg stands at a party, or throwing back tequila shots at the bar, every facet of his life revolves around getting plowed. You're not a Mormon or anything, but every time you try to keep up with him, you end up nearing alcohol poisoning, not to mention a hangover that lasts for two days.

3. **PUPPY LOVE:** Even though you've only hooked up with him a few times, you get the feeling that he's slightly smitten with you. Maybe it's because all the girls he usually hangs out with are young and insecure and you come off sophisticated and self-confident, or maybe he just assumes that since you're

older, you automatically want a boyfriend and he's more than willing to volunteer. Either way, it's really sweet to have someone cook you breakfast in bed (even if it is Pop-Tarts and Yoo-Hoo).

4. **EASY TARGET:** You knew your friends wouldn't let this one slide without at least a little snickering, but you never thought *they* would end up being the most immature part of the hookup. They never miss an opportunity to ask you how much your baby-sitting job pays. Normally you'd be pissed off at them for acting like such jerks, but it's obvious that they're just jealous that you are having so much damn fun with your younger boy toy.

MORNING-AFTER ATTIRE: Not applicable—there's no way you'd ever sleep in his bed, since the last time his sheets were changed was when his mom did it for him during Parents' Weekend (which was over a month ago).

WHY IT ENDS: He starts pledging a fraternity and they lock him in a basement for a month.

ONE HOOKUP, TWO VERY DIFFERENT SCHEDULES

Remember how in college you would sleep in late, hang out with your friends in the student center, and party until the sun came up? Seems like only yesterday. Well, for him that *was* yesterday. Here's a look at the different lives you lead.

TIME	YOU	HIM
6:30 A.M.	Hit snooze button	Snoozes
6:35 A.M.	Drag ass out of bed, brush teeth, put on workout attire and sleepwalk to the gym	Scratches ass while still sleeping in bed
6:45– 7:30 A.M.	Spend forty-five minutes on the elliptical machine in a desperate attempt to keep ass small and cute, despite scarfing down half the deluxe appetizer platter at bar last night with boy toy	Spends forty-five minutes dreaming about your ass
9:30 A.M.– 12:30 P.M.	**9:30-10:30:** Get to work, drink first cup of coffee, reply to fifteen e-mails, return six voice mail messages **10:30-12:30:** Sort through inbox, file status reports, prepare memo for this afternoon's meeting, browse Shopbop.com, order Chinese for lunch	**12:30:** Wakes and bakes

TIME	YOU	HIM
1:00–3:00 P.M.	**1:00-2:00:** Struggle not to fall asleep during "Increasing Productivity in the Workplace" meeting **2:00-3:00:** Drink second cup of coffee and work on twenty-page Excel document	Falls asleep during "Intro to Computing"
4:20 P.M.	Run to the newsstand to pick up M&Ms	Skips class to celebrate his favorite time of the day by smoking a joint and playing Ultimate Frisbee on the quad
6:30–8:30 P.M.	Meet your friends for dinner; have one glass of wine	Heats up a bowl of Easy Mac; has one can of beer
9:00–11:00 P.M.	Put on pjs, watch reruns of *Friends,* and start dozing off on the couch	Puts on his "Jesus is my Homeboy" T-shirt and invites fifteen friends over to start pre-gaming
2:00 A.M.	Zzzz . . .	Calls the hot older chick he's hooking up with (duh, you) and gets her voice mail. Leaves the following message: "Heeeey babe, it's me, just calling to see what you're doing, maybe I can stop by later. Umm . . . what time is it? Oh shit, it's like two in the morning. Well, you're probably sleeping but [incoherent rambling] . . . Okay, talk to you later."

TYPECASTING

ACT YOUR AGE, NOT YOUR SHOE SIZE

If a Pass-the-Sippy-Cup hookup is making you nostalgic for the good old days, here are some reasons why it's great to be your age:

- You've finally figured out how to pronounce Moët & Chandon.

- You actually enjoy getting carded at bars.

- You either live alone or with someone you actually like, so you don't have to put up with any more bipolar, anorexic, manic-depressive, kleptomaniac, nymphomaniac roommates.

- You don't have to explain to your parents why your Visa bill is creeping toward five digits.

- You never have to pull another all-nighter writing a psychology paper that needs a hypothesis, an experiment, a control group, and five other mandatory elements (none of which you really understand).

- You have actual steam to blow off at happy hour.

- You finally understand Dennis Miller's jokes.

- You have your own business cards, which makes giving guys your number so much simpler.

- You have a reason to buy all the cute working-girl ensembles at Banana Republic.

- You don't (usually) drink until you puke anymore.

THE BEST BUD TRYST
When Platonic Turns Erotic

THE SCENARIO: Maybe you two met in high school when your respective moms forced you to join the debate team (to pad those college resumes, of course), and you bonded over a mutual apathy for the major issues affecting the world. Or maybe you lived on the same floor freshman year, drank away the nights with cheap keg beer, and spent your days sitting together in the student union, eating until the point of near-explosion (thanks to a fully financed meal card). Or you found each other at work—instant soul mates among the maze of cubicles—and wasted time nine to five instant messaging about your latest "projects" (*How does the sum function in Excel work?*), what that tramp in accounting was wearing (*Does she own a bra?*), and the finer points of your boss's hair (*toupee or plugs?*). No matter how you met, you were friends (meaning no hanky-panky) until a moment of weakness/loneliness/drunkenness/horniness took over, transforming your relationship from platonic to erotic faster than you could say "cheesy Meg Ryan movie."

HIM, IN A NUTSHELL: While you probably have tons of different guy friends, the Best Bud Tryst usually falls into one of the following categories: the old standby or the pressure cooker.

The old standby is cotton or baby terry: comfortingly warm and uncomplicated. You've never thought about him in a sexual way, but he'd do anything for you, and you'd do anything for him. He's your perfect guy—minus the chemistry. You might have tried to set him up (unsuccessfully) with one of your girlfriends (he was too good for her, anyway). But one night something just *happened* between the two of you, leaving you more than a little confused. Could it be that you actually like him in that way? Or was it just the fact that he's always there for you?

While the old standby is the boy next door, the pressure cooker is a different story—he's the really *hot* boy next door. Everyone lives for him: Girls fall at his feet; guys think he's cool. You thank your lucky stars you can use him as a "rescue date" for weddings, birthday parties, and other embarrassing family functions. On more than one occasion, you've suppressed a smile (and felt guilty about it later on) when a waiter or salesperson mistook you two for a couple. After all, the pressure cooker has always regarded you as the friend he could really trust—not just another girl who was waiting in line for her turn to hook up with him.

THE UPSIDE: He likes you for your mind.

> **EXAMPLE:** He's impressed by the fact that you can tell the Olsen twins apart.

BUYER BEWARE: Since you know each other so well, there's no mystery left in your relationship.

> **EXAMPLE:** You held a vigil with him after his pet iguana "passed on" (and didn't laugh out loud).

IDENTIFYING FEATURES OF THE BEST BUD TRYST

1. **THE GRACE PERIOD:** Just being on your buddy list doesn't automatically make him your friend. In order to be a true Best Bud Tryst, you guys need to have a platonic history—one year is usually a safe minimum. You hang out together. You have mutual friends. You have seen each other at your worst. (Check out the quiz on page 103 to figure out what type of friends you are and therefore how well the two of you will fare in the face of booty.)

2. **THE "ICK" FACTOR:** After the hookup, you find yourself on a wild roller-coaster ride of emotion. In a matter of minutes you go from elation ("Yay! He might be the one!") to shock and horror ("I can't believe I made out with him. I know exactly where that mouth has been."). These highs and lows only get worse as you have more time to sit around and really think about what happened. Suddenly, all of the gross things he's ever done in your presence—like the time he tried to teach you how to pee standing up—flood your mind with embarrassing imagery.

3. **BUSYBODIES:** Everyone loves a juicy story, and two friends plus a dash of booty equals major scandal. Once your social circle gets wind of your hookup, you won't hear the end of it for a long, long time. Soon you can't even go into the ladies' room at the bar without someone accosting you and saying, "Ohmygod, I can't believe you hooked up with him," or "Ohmygod, I always knew you two would end up together. Aren't you *buggin' out?* Call me if you need to talk!" Riiiight. You wish all of your gossip-starved buds would leave you alone and go back to watching *Entertainment Tonight.*

4. **THE AGONY OF THE ECSTASY:** Now that the deed is done, you face that scary moment of truth (gulp) when you have to face your friend. All sorts of questions rush through your head: Will your friendship end? Will you fall madly in love and ride off into the sunset together? Or will he go back to giving you noogies? The stakes are high, and you are afraid that it could take a long time before things will get back to the way they were pre-booty.

MORNING-AFTER ATTIRE: Your jeans and the flannel shirt that he wore every single day of high school during his grunge phase

POP QUIZ: HOW DEEP IS YOUR LOVE?
What Kind of Friendship Do You Have?

Okay, so there are friends, and then there are true-blue, friends till the end. How you and your guy fare through the uncharted waters of hooking up depends a lot on the strength of your friendship. Not sure if you two are genuine besties or just really friendly drinking buddies? This quiz can help you out. Here's how it works: Give yourself 100 points to start with. For each question, choose one scenario that best fits your relationship. Add or subtract the points according to your answers.

1. He's seen you puke. (+1)

   He's held your hair while you've puked. (+5)

   He's helped you into your pajamas after you puked and swore that he didn't look at your boobs. (+10)

2. You've smoked weed together. (+1)

   You've bought a bong together. (+5)

   You've fought over whose house it should stay at. (+10)

3. You've made him take a ballroom dance class with you. (+10)

   You've drunkenly bumped and grinded on the dance floor at a club. (-5)

   You've danced kinda close and felt a little poke comin' through. (-15)

4. He's forwarded you Internet porn. (+5)

   He's shown you his Internet porn collection. (+2)

   He Photoshopped your face onto Jenna Jameson's body. (-20)

5. He's seen you without makeup. (+1)

   He's seen you in a bathing suit. (+5)

   He's "accidentally" walked in while you were changing and seen you in your birthday suit. (-10) (Minus 10 more points if he didn't immediately cover his eyes.)

6. You've gone to the mall together. (+1)

   You've gone purse shopping for his mother. (+5)

   He's held your purse while you were shopping. (+20)

7. He's looked at your baby photos. (+5)

   He's looked at your high school yearbooks. (+1)

   You've caught him looking at your cleavage. (-10)

8. You have inside jokes. (+5)

   You've made a pinky swear. (+10)

   You finish each other's sentences. (+20)

9. He knows your middle name. (+5)

   He knows the names of your siblings. (+10)

   He knows the names of the children that you will one day have together.[8] (-20)

10. He usually likes your boyfriends. (+5)

   He thinks some of your exes weren't good enough for you (and was right). (+10)

   He's assaulted one of your boyfriends. (-20)

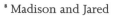
madison & jared

---

[8] Madison and Jared

165–200 points   *Winnie Cooper and Kevin Arnold*

You are best friends in a grew-up-down-the-street-from-each-other, *Wonder Years* kind of way. If you had a tree next to your bedroom window, he would probably climb up it to hang out with you. Since you guys are like brother and sister, you probably shouldn't continue hooking up. Frankly, it's kind of nasty. But fear not. While this bout with booty might result in some temporary awkwardness, it won't drive you two apart. In fact, not much could.

101–164 points   *Joey and Rachel*

While you have a solid friendship, there's still some mystery there (meaning he's never farted in front of you). How will a makeout session affect your relationship? Well, you should do okay, as long as one of you is willing to take the first steps to ease the morning-after tension (and no, getting really drunk and making out again is probably not the best way to go about this). Bite the bullet, call him up, and have a good laugh.

Your relationship is a lot like being on a seesaw with someone who is a bit more robust than you are—it's very unbalanced. While you like him, he obviously *likes you* likes you. Ewww. In this case of a lopsided friendship, a hookup will mean very different things to each of the parties involved. You'll think it was merely a lapse in judgment, and he'll probably be under the impression that it was the first step down the aisle. Stop stringing him along and just let it go before someone gets hurt. You're playing with fire.

HOW IT ENDS: The Best Bud Tryst has the potential to end in three different ways.

ENDING 1: You'll realize that you are totally in love and live happily ever after. (Barf!)

ENDING 2: You'll feel so awkward that your friendship essentially ends (scary, but it happens).

ENDING 3: You'll have a good laugh over your mutual lapse in judgment and vow that you're better off as friends.

THAT'S WHAT FRIENDS ARE FOR
WHY GUYS MAKE GREAT BUDS

So, let's say your Best Bud Tryst ended on such a sour note that you and your friend aren't quite on speaking terms. Always keep this in mind: Finding a good guy friend is as rare as finding the perfect strapless bra. Here are some incentives to get you to end the standoff, pick up the phone, and bring your BFF back into your life:

1. **MR. FIX-IT:** You're not exactly a damsel in distress, but it's nice to have a stronger set of arms around to help you move your endless supply of Ikea furniture into a new (sixth-floor walk-up) apartment. A guy friend will gladly do the grunt work—for a six-pack.

2. **A DOSE OF TRUTH SERUM:** Unlike your girlfriends, who force a smile when you parade out of your bedroom in a way unflattering top, he'll immediately say, "Um, why don't you try your red sweater? I hear it's supposed to get really cold out tonight, *and* I can totally see your nips in what you're wearing right now."

3. **SIX DEGREES OF SEPARATION:** He's a cool guy, so he's bound to have cool guy friends he can introduce you to, right? Exactly. The added bonus of this little setup is that your friend will presort his pals into two groups: the decent guys (dateable) and the assholes (steer clear). This

will save you the trauma of finding out the hard way that "Mr. Nice Guy" is really "Mr. Whips and Chains."

4. **ARM CANDY:** Like we mentioned before, a good guy friend will be around if you need a last-minute date for your cousin Sal's wedding. Having him in tow forces your relatives to keep their embarrassing comments to themselves. (Remember when you showed up dateless to Uncle Danny's retirement party and your ninety-year-old nana asked your mom if you were a "Lebanese"?)

5. **BIG BROTHER:** He knows exactly when to swoop in and save you from the sleazy fifty-year-old insurance salesmen who circle bars like hawks. All you have to utter is something like, "Well, *my boyfriend* really loves that movie" and your guy will be at your side faster than Larry of State Farm can say, "Can I buy you a vodka and cran?"

6. **WARM AND COMFY:** When hanging out with a guy friend, there's no need to stifle a burp or sit with your legs crossed. Casting judgment is not a part of his MO, so you can be yourself around him. Take our advice and drop the delicate flower act. He'd rather you polished off the rest of the buffalo wings than sit around and pretend that ladies never poo-poo.

7. **HOW THE OTHER HALF LIVES:** We girls hate to admit the fact that male behavior occasionally baffles us. For instance, what's so great about Alyssa Milano, how

does Staind sell records, and is it really necessary to wear a sweater, a button-down, *and* a T-shirt? A close guy friend can provide insight into all of these mysteries and so many more.

8. **PHOTOGRAPHIC MEMORY:** Your guy pal tends to remember little details—even when you thought he wasn't paying attention. (Okay, so sometimes his observations are a bit too honest, but you forgave him for that time he shouted, *"What did you do to your hair?"* when you tried to emulate the "Jennifer Aniston" back in 1995.) Thanks to his powerful memory, you're always guaranteed to get a phone call on your birthday from a guy who's not related to you.

9. **A CALMING FORCE:** Whenever you're sweating the small stuff, a surrogate big brother can help keep you in check. Next time your monster of a boss gets on your case about missing a deadline, rather than freaking out and worrying that she is out to get you, take a cue from your guy friend: Give your boss the "middle finger eye scratch" that you perfected in sixth grade, and forget about it.

10. **ALL EYES ON YOU:** You always get to be the prettier one. Enough said.

OOPS, I DID IT AGAIN
The Ex-Boyfriend

THE SCENARIO: Your best friend casually mentions that your ex will be making a cameo at the bar tonight. "Whatever," you say as you speed dial the salon to schedule an emergency blow-out, bikini wax, and mani-pedi appointment, "I am soooo over him." Clearly. When he walks into the bar you spend 4.5 minutes pretending you don't see him, 3.5 minutes reapplying your lip gloss, and 2.5 minutes flirting with some random dude in an attempt to remind your ex what a hot piece of ass you are. Finally, you work your way over to him (it's not desperate to approach him first; you did wait a full ten minutes) and say the line you've rehearsed in the mirror since you broke up six months ago: "Hey, how are you?" After three shots, one "Pour Some Sugar on Me," and a powwow in the girls' room where you swear to your friends that he is being soooo nice, you go home with the same guy who sent you straight to therapy with a lifetime prescription for Prozac.

HIM, IN A NUTSHELL: While every girl has a unique ex-boyfriend saga, it's probably safe to say that yours was traumatizing and left you doubting your mental stability. It's likely that when you first met, he was completely smitten with you. He may have sent you witty e-mails at work, called you whenever something remotely funny happened, and took you out to dinner to fab restaurants. On Valentine's Day, he most likely sent you a dozen red roses. For your birthday you probably got a cheesy necklace with a heart pendant. He may have even schlepped you to his grandmother's ninetieth birthday party and proudly introduced you to all his (boring) relatives. You were so sure that he was a keeper. Then seemingly out of nowhere, Mr. I've-never-felt-this-way-about-anyone-before morphed into Mr. I'm-just-not-ready-to-be-with-one-person. Oh, and of course he still wants to be friends.

THE UPSIDE: Since he already knows what gets you all hot and bothered, you're pretty much guaranteed a good time.

> **EXAMPLE:** He won't try to spank you (unless, of course, that's the kind of thing you enjoy).

BUYER BEWARE: It's obvious—he's your ex, therefore he's an asshole.

> **EXAMPLE:** His favorite new line is, "Well, technically I'm not your boyfriend, so . . ."

IDENTIFYING FEATURES OF THE "OOPS, I DID IT AGAIN" HOOKUP

1. **UNIVERSAL INDIFFERENCE:** For your friends, coworkers, relatives, and hairstylist, this recycled love affair is like watching reruns of 90210. They already know how this played-out story line is going to end, so they pretty much just tune out as you ramble on and on about your "situation."

2. **COMFORT FACTOR:** Hooking up with your ex is the equivalent of traveling to Europe and scarfing down McDonald's for every meal: It's easy and available, but not all that exciting. If it's a matter of being afraid to try something new, just remember the first time someone forced you to eat sushi. Now you're ordering spicy tuna rolls like nobody's business.

3. **DON'T ASK, DON'T TELL POLICY:** While it's clear that you two are not a couple anymore, hooking up with other people is not to be discussed—which is fine, since neither one of you has the balls to come right out and ask the other if they are seeing anyone "special."

4. **YOU'RE ONLY CHEATING YOURSELF:** If you've ever gobbled up an entire bag of Wow! chips and thought you were getting away with murder, then you may also remember the unpleasant physical ramifications that followed shortly after. The point is, don't think you can hook up with your ex and not have to deal with the emotional side effects that will most definitely ensue.

MORNING-AFTER ATTIRE: The ugly sweatpants that you kept at his place and never bothered to ask for after you broke up, along with the sweater you bought him for his birthday that still has the tags on it

THE PROS AND CONS OF HOOKING UP WITH YOUR EX

PROS	CONS
You don't have to pretend to like his friends.	He still doesn't pretend to like your friends.
His mom still thinks you're the best thing that ever happened to him.	Your mom still thinks he's an asshole.
You've lost five pounds since he broke up with you.	You gain six while hooking up with him.
He hasn't found someone else.	Neither have you.
He still has your toothbrush at his place.	You don't know who else has used it since the breakup.
He knows what your favorite date restaurant is.	He doesn't take you there anymore.
If you kiss another guy, you're not cheating on him.	If he kisses another girl, he's not cheating on you (this time).
He hasn't changed.	He hasn't changed.

WHY IT ENDS: You stay in one night and watch Pamela Anderson's *E! True Hollywood Story* and it hits way too close to home. The next day you stop returning his calls.

TEN WAYS TO BID HIM ADIEU FOR GOOD

Okay, so maybe kicking your ex-boyfriend habit is easier said than done. Perhaps you need to send him on his way—in grand style. Whether you want to drive him so crazy that he vows never to speak to you again (you should be so lucky) or just get it over with and give him the heave-ho, here's a list of ways to make sure he'll go away for good:

1. Put his picture on Match.com under the "Men Seeking Men" section. Then accuse him of cheating on you and living a lie.

2. Ask him to join you at a couples retreat so the two of you can form an everlasting emotional bond.

3. Encourage him to pursue his dream of joining the Peace Corps.

4. Sell all the stuff he ever gave you on eBay and use the profits to buy your teacup Yorkie a new cashmere hoodie.

5. Call him every day for a week at 6:32 A.M. to ask him what he's thinking about and where he thinks your relationship is going.

6. Have your best friend send him sexy text messages, then "catch" him in the act.

7. Blast "Bye Bye Bye" into the phone every time he calls you.

8. Customize an engagement ring on the DeBeers Web site and forward him the link with the subject line, "Start saving for the next two months, baby!"

9. Change your outgoing voice mail message to say, "Hi, you've reached [insert your name, his name, and your dog's name]."

10. Send him a cookie cake that says "It's Over" in pretty pink icing.

PUTTING IN OVERTIME
Coworker Canoodling

THE SCENARIO: Since your last name isn't Hilton, you actually have to work for a living. Monday through Friday, you wake up to the buzz of an alarm clock, get dressed in sensible career-girl clothes, and shuffle off to eight hours in a cubicle. Even if you like your job—or are one of the lucky few who love it—the hum of the fluorescent lights and hollering of your boss over speakerphone gets really old, really quick. So in an attempt to spice things up, your coworkers treat the workplace like an extension of college (it helps that everyone in your department is still pretty young). They fill one another's e-mail inboxes with dirty forwards, play intramural sports, and stage a weekly drinking ritual: the coveted happy hour. While the gossip is amusing, you steer clear of actually becoming a topic of water cooler conversation—until one evening when your cubemate convinces you to join everyone at the corner pub for one drink. You swing by just to say hi. Three tequila shots and three pints of beer later, you find yourself liplocked with Jon, the hottie in accounting, behind the Ms. Pacman machine.

HIM, IN A NUTSHELL: You really don't know too much about him except that he has a loud phone voice and he won the office March Madness pool two years in a row. While you've never seen him out of his work clothes (usually a bright blue button-down and charcoal-gray trousers), you are absolutely positive that he'd look great in something a little more, um, comfortable.

THE UPSIDE: You have a little drama to keep work exciting.

> **EXAMPLE:** A trip to the bathroom becomes a major event—especially if you have to walk past his cube.

BUYER BEWARE: Keep in mind that when things end, you'll have to see this guy every day at work (unless you want to transfer to your company's Anchorage bureau).

> **EXAMPLE:** Every time you are in a meeting together, you'll be reminded that he has seen your boobs.

MORNING-AFTER ATTIRE: Post-rendezvous, a working girl like you is spotted in tailored black trousers, pointy pumps, and a smart button-down—with her employee identification badge still clipped to her belt loop.

IDENTIFYING FEATURES OF THE PUTTING-IN-OVERTIME HOOKUP

1. **ADRENALINE RUSH:** Who needs to base jump or skydive when you're having an illicit office affair? The thrill of almost getting caught eases the excruciating boredom associated with creating expense reports.

2. **THE TELEPHONE GAME:** In an office setting, rumors spread like wildfire (and everyone is convinced that *they* have the inside scoop). Let's say you had a PG-rated hookup. In a moment of weakness you let your secret slip to Julie in marketing, who

turns around and tells Ron in logistics that you slept with your hottie coworker, who tells Donna the nighttime receptionist that you're having his love child. Before you know it, the girls in accounts payable are planning your baby shower.

3. **SEXY SECRETARY:** Suddenly your usual day-to-evening look morphs into an evening-to-evening look, complete with tight turtlenecks, sexy (yet tasteful) fishnets, and skinny heels, which kill your feet but look utterly fabulous. You'd rather lose your right arm than be caught dashing out of the office wearing running shoes with a skirt.

4. **EMPLOYEE OF THE MONTH:** Suddenly Ms. I-Keep-Work-and-Personal-Life-Separate is putting in extra hours at all of the drunken office social functions in order to spend more time with him. You've even started doing the unthinkable: playing shortstop in the company softball league.

CORPORATE CULTURE
A LOOK AT HOW HOOKUPS HAPPEN IN VARIOUS WORKPLACES

THE SERVICE INDUSTRY	THE CUBE SLAVES	THE DO-GOODERS	THE ARTISTES
Hot Jobs			
Waiters, bartenders, and anyone else who can eat and drink on the job	Number crunchers, sales reps, and anyone who wears a headset phone and runs the risk of developing carpal tunnel syndrome	Social workers, environmental activists, counselors— people who love people but hate Wal-Mart	Actors, designers, stylists, and other "creative types" who throw tantrums when the intern brings them French Hazelnut with cream even though he's been told a million times that they can't digest dairy, goddammit
What Makes These Jobs Havens for Hooking Up			
Crazy hours, stressful atmosphere, easy access to a fully stocked bar	Boredom—you can only play Minesweeper for so long.	While you might be able to rage against the machine, raging against the hormones is a losing battle.	Lots of "emotionally available" coworkers (aka people who let their bipolar disorder go untreated)

THE SERVICE INDUSTRY	THE CUBE SLAVES	THE DO-GOODERS	THE ARTISTES
Your Partner in Crime			
The overnight cook	Jon in accounting	The Greenpeace hottie who shares office space with the progressive grassroots organization that you work for	The art director who wears all black and smokes Euro cigarettes
Where You First Hooked Up			
After your shift, at the bar next door to the bar where you work	Bennigan's happy hour	In the paddy wagon during a WTO protest	After *The Vagina Monologues*
Most Embarrassing Moment			
You get locked in the walk-in cooler during a make-out session.	You mistakenly send a tell-all e-mail to "Marketing Staff" instead of to your friend Mark.	He finds out that you eat veal.	You go to his gallery opening and notice that his painting, *Untitled Nude*, bears a striking resemblance to you.

WHY IT ENDS: Your boss makes you attend one of those "sexual harassment in the workplace" meetings—and by you, we mean only you. You get the picture and quickly nix your late nights at the office.

TAKE THE HEAT OFF OF YOU

The office gossip trolls will definitely find out about your failed affair. In order to redirect the glare of the spotlight from you and onto someone or something else, you're going to have to stage a better PR blitz than when Janet Jackson flashed her nipple. Here are six brilliant office scandals to instigate:

○ Repeatedly steal a coworker's stapler. Leave a ransom note.

○ Fill the tampon machine in the ladies' bathroom with gumballs.

○ After the tech department warns you about an e-mail virus with the subject heading "hugs4U," "accidentally" open it and shut down your office's entire network indefinitely.

○ Send Bev, the middle-aged office manager (who owns six cats, has ten years of *All My Children* on tape, and hasn't had a man since George Bush Sr. was in office) an e-mail that simply says: "What's up with [insert the names of two unsuspecting coworkers]?" Watch havoc ensue: She'll definitely get the gossip going on this brand-new scandal.

- Buy two dozen donuts and leave them in the kitchen area with a sign that reads, "Try the New Low-Carb Krispy Kremes!!"

- Introduce the nymphomaniac in human resources to the geeky hornball in marketing, then "catch" them having sex in the supply closet.

THE CHEATER
The Guy with a Girlfriend

THE SCENARIO: When you first meet him, he seems too good to be true—laid-back, super confident, and genuinely interested in what you have to say. And after hooking up with him a few times, you start to think the unthinkable—he'd make the perfect boyfriend. Unfortunately, he neglects to mention that he *is* the perfect boyfriend—someone else's.

When he does get around to letting you know that he's "kind of seeing someone," you flip out and demand to know why he didn't tell you right off the bat. His response: "Well, it's not like you asked or anything." But what's worse than his lack of guilt is your lack of guilt. You know that it completely violates girl code to hook up with someone else's boyfriend, but through his web of lies, half-truths, and fabrications, you manage to rationalize your appalling behavior by believing him when he says that he and "girl X" have advanced to the final stages of relationship decay: the "we've agreed to see other people" phase.

HIM, IN A NUTSHELL: Since he already has easy booty access at home, he feels no need to pull desperate moves like using pickup lines to get a girl's attention. Instead, he'll approach you in a casual manner that makes you wonder if he's hitting on you or just looking for someone to talk to. And although you're convinced it's the former, he maintains that it was all in the name of good conversation. The Cheater thinks he's a gift to all the ladies of the world. Despite the fact that he already has a girlfriend, he feels no need to take himself off the market. Why bother? There's enough of him to go around. He uses convoluted—albeit intriguing—logic to justify getting it on with someone other than his girlfriend. (*It's not cheating if we don't kiss on the lips. Uh-huh.*)

THE UPSIDE: You know exactly where this little tryst is going—nowhere.

> **EXAMPLE:** If you have a boyfriend, then the Cheater is the perfect person to cheat on your boy with.

BUYER BEWARE: At the end of the day, you're the frites and she's the steak (and what guy goes for fries over a nice cut of filet?).

> **EXAMPLE:** When she catches a cold, he runs home with a can of chicken soup. When you catch a cold, he tells you to call him when you're not contagious.

IDENTIFYING FEATURES OF THE CHEATER HOOKUP

1. **DENIAL ISN'T A RIVER IN EGYPT:** In the case of a Cheater hookup, it's your new frame of mind. While you know very well that there's definitely someone else in his life, you make a very conscious decision to pretend that she doesn't exist. You don't ask questions, you don't think about it; you just cup your hands over your ears and shout, "La, la, la!" whenever you hear her name.

2. **KARMA KICKBACK:** It's not your fault if you hook up with a guy who went to painstaking lengths to hide the fact that he has a girlfriend (what are you supposed to do—submit everyone you meet to a polygraph test?). But if you keep coming back for more even after he's come clean about his romantic status, watch out. Pardon the use of a cliché, but what goes around really does come around.

3. **JURY OF YOUR PEERS:** At first your friends try to break it to you gently. "Ummm, I'm pretty sure you're not the only person he's hooking up with." But when you completely ignore their warnings and go back for seconds—and thirds—with him, they decide to put it a little more bluntly: "Please stop being a ho-bag before someone gets hurt."

4. **THE NOT-SO-EX-GIRLFRIEND:** He insists she's finally out of the picture, but it's more like she's out of town. When his girlfriend (or ex-girlfriend, or whatever he calls her) finds out that you're making nice with him while she was visiting her sick grandmother, you'd better get ready for some Jerry Springer-esque hysterics. Remember: Even though it takes two to tango, at the end of the day he's her beloved boyfriend and you're just the trash who be messin' with her man.

MORNING-AFTER ATTIRE: Ha! Right—like he'd ever let you sleep over at his place. It's more like he elbows you in the ribs when he sees you're starting to fall asleep and pretty much forces you to go home at 4 A.M.

THE BULLSHIT DECODER

The Cheater's got more lines than the DMV. Here, we decipher the double-talk he uses to wrap you around his little, um, finger. . . .

WHAT HE SAYS	WHAT HE MEANS
I don't have time for a relationship right now.	I have a girlfriend *and* I'm hooking up with someone else. I don't know how long I can keep this up before I get caught.
Well, I was dating someone, but we've decided that we should start seeing other people.	I've decided that I need to see some other boobies—Skinamax just isn't doing it for me anymore.
I'm still friends with my ex-girlfriend.	She's my baby's mama.
We *were* doing the long-distance thing, but it wasn't working out.	My girlfriend went to visit her parents for the weekend.
We're not technically together.	She hasn't moved in with me—yet.
She means nothing to me.	Neither do you.
But she would be *crushed* if I broke up with her right now.	Why would I ever end it with someone who puts up with all of my bullshit?
I want to spend time with you, but things are so crazy right now.	Isn't it crazy that polygamy isn't more universally accepted?

HOW IT ENDS: The Cheater Hookup could end in one of two ways.

ENDING 1: He decides he loves the girlfriend he has been cheating on and somehow manages to blame you for almost breaking them up.

ENDING 2: She wages a war against you that makes the conflict in the Middle East look like a playground scuffle, and you're forced to move to another city or transfer to another school.

HE'S NOT REALLY BUSY AT WORK, HE'S REALLY BUSY HAVING A GIRLFRIEND IF:

○ You hardly ever hang out at his apartment.

○ On the rare occasion that you did hook up at his place (and you scrounged around in his bathroom), you noticed that he didn't have a box of condoms—but he did have a box of tampons.

○ He has a picture in his wallet of him with a girl he's hugging a little too tightly to be his sister.

○ You only see him on off hours—like 2 A.M. to 4 A.M.— and he never calls you to get together on Friday nights (known in relationship land as "dinner and a movie night").

- He programs you into his phone under your initials instead of your full name.

- His phone rings constantly and he never answers it, but he compulsively checks his voice mail.

- He text messages you more frequently than he calls you.

- He always picks bars that are nowhere near his apartment.

- His friends act a little strange around you—i.e., they smirk at one another when you walk into the room.

- He disappears for weekends at a time and turns off his cell phone.

GIRLS GONE WILD
The Spring Break Fling

THE SCENARIO: Whether you just finished midterms and want to embark on the rite of passage like every college student, or you're sick of freezing temperatures and seek refuge in a sunny destination, spring break is to hooking up as fat-free, sugar-free fro-yo is to an anorexic: paradise. That's because every spring breaker has the same basic game plan: get tan, get drunk, and get laid. To reiterate: Spring break is not the time to don a muumuu-like cover-up, have a glass of wine at dinner, or meet your next boyfriend. Rather, it's a time to flaunt your tan bod in a barely there halter top, drink a pitcher of margaritas for dinner, and make out with someone else's boyfriend.

HIM, IN A NUTSHELL: It seems that practically every guy you meet on spring break will be named Dave, Mike, or Brian. He's spent every day for the past three months lifting at the gym, shaved his upper body to enhance the results of countless bench presses, and packed an economy-size box of condoms just in case. Dave/Mike/Brian is a marketing major and is probably joined by all seventeen of his frat brothers, who, oddly, are all named Dave, Mike, or Brian. You meet him on the dance floor at the local disco,* where the two of you work up quite a sweat dancing to hits from the late 1990s. You've been making out to Naughty By Nature's "O.P.P." when he says, "Let's get out of here." Before you know it, you're full-fledged hooking up with him on the disgusting floral print hotel bedspread, just like hundreds of spring breakers have done before you. Ewww.

---

* You can only call a bar a "disco" on spring break.

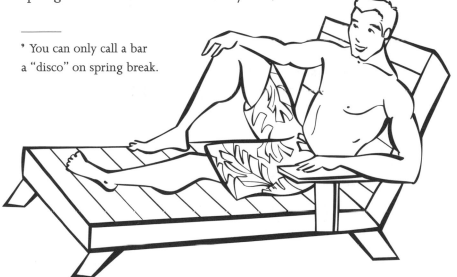

TYPECASTING

THE UPSIDE: It's just like your bikini when you played in the waves after one too many cocktails: no strings attached. Since this hookup is based purely on fun, you don't have to worry about him calling you, let alone if he's going to wake up when you leave in the morning.

> **EXAMPLE:** He nods hello to you at the pool and you feel like he's stalking you.

BUYER BEWARE: Even if you really like him, there's nothing you can do about it, because a relationship born out of a spring break hookup is like a cloned sheep—it's just not natural.

> **EXAMPLE:** He'll never bring the 2002 Cancun Wet T-Shirt Champion home to meet his mother.

IDENTIFYING FEATURES OF THE GIRLS-GONE-WILD HOOKUP

1. **WHERE'S WALDO?:** Locating Prince Charming the night after you hook up is a harder task than getting him to give you pesos for the cab ride home the next morning. The odds are not in your favor. You find yourself in a giant foam party

packed with eight hundred Dave/Mike/Brian look-alikes, who are all shirtless and twirling their glow sticks to the beat of the techno music.

2. **ROCK-BOTTOM STANDARDS:** Normally you wouldn't hook up with Vinny from Staten Island, who is 5'4" and sports a skintight black T-shirt and a faux bling-bling Italian horn. But then again, you don't normally drink three margaritas, four shots of tequila, and a vodka tonic *before* you make it to the bar.

3. **HOLIDAY RULES APPLY:** You can do anything that nice girls don't do because spring break is a vacuum. In fact, none of your friends were even fazed by the fact that they walked in on you getting freaky with Dave/Mike/Brian, Vinny, and some chick named Tiffany.

4. **MISS PRUDEY PANTS:** If you don't hook up with at least three random dudes, you feel oddly nun-like and disappointed by your lack of sluttiness. Your parents would be so proud.

MORNING-AFTER ATTIRE: Your halter top, miniskirt, one hoop earring, one shoe, and a huge hickey on your neck

BIKINIS AND BEER
A LOOK AT THE MOST POPULAR SPRING BREAK DESTINATIONS

Destination	CANCUN	DAYTONA	VEGAS
Where You Stay	The Oasis	A Howard Johnson's	The Hard Rock Hotel and Casino
Who You'll Meet	A boy in a backwards visor with a shaved chest, a seashell choker, and a tribal tattoo around his bicep	A boy who drives a pickup truck and brings his own Styrofoam cooler and beer bong to the beach	A boy in a black button-down shirt, Diesel jeans, and a diamond Rolex
Nightlife	Doing body shots and dancing on top of the bar at Señor Frogs	Cruising Atlantic Avenue in a rented Mustang convertible	Pleading with the doorman to let you into Ghostbar
Drink of Choice	Anything in a yard glass	Any beer that advertises during NFL games	Anything in a martini glass
Attire	A bikini top and a denim mini	A tube top to show off your brand-new pink rhinestone belly ring	Low-rise jeans, a cleavage-baring top, and snakeskin pumps

Destination	CANCUN	DAYTONA	VEGAS
Beauty Must-Haves	A Brazilian bikini wax and anti-frizz serum	Body glitter and acrylic nails	Spray-on tan and a pedicure
Preferred Drugs	Ecstasy and Immodium AD	Oxycotin (aka "Hillbilly Heroin") and steroids	Cocaine and No-Doz
Overused Phrase	"What goes on in Cancun stays in Cancun."	"Show me your tits."	"Vegas, baby!"
Highlight	Grinding by the pool with some meathead on the MTV Spring Break set	Making it on *Girls Gone Wild 2005*	Winning twelve dollars at blackjack—enough to pay for one Cosmo at the bar
Low Point	Getting Montezuma's Revenge and having to use the bathroom at Fat Tuesday's	Getting a tattoo of a dolphin on your ankle while you were drunk	Getting married to a guy you met an hour ago

WHY IT ENDS: The sun comes up.

WHAT GOES ON AT SPRING BREAK DOESN'T NECESSARILY GO ON IN ST. PAUL
(OR WHEREVER YOU SPEND THE OTHER FIFTY-ONE WEEKS OF THE YEAR)

AT HOME . . .	ON SPRING BREAK . . .
You have three classes in one day.	You have a threesome.
You study until four in the morning.	You have a foursome.
As a favor, you lend your notes to that cute guy in Bio.	You pretend that you are too drunk to "return the favor."
You eat tater tots at the dining hall.	You flash your ta-tas for the *Girls Gone Wild* cameras.
You drink Sex on the Beach.	You have sex on the beach.
You sleep until lunch.	You have a make-out session before lunch.
You bust your booty on the elliptical.	You enter a booty-shaking contest—and win.
You have a 3.2 GPA.	You have a .32 BAC.
You hooked up with him until your interest started to fade.	You hooked up with him until his tan started to fade.
You leave your term paper on ethics and morals with your T.A.	You leave your ethics and morals at the border.
You cover your body with a fleece and a down jacket to stay warm.	You cover your body with a teeny tube dress to look hot.

THE JOEY BUTTAFUOCO
The Guy Who Drives You Crazy—Literally

THE SCENARIO: You consider yourself to be a fairly rational girl. You don't flip the bird when someone cuts you off in traffic. You try to be polite when telemarketers interrupt your must-see TV to babble on and on about the latest advances in vacuum cleaner technology. And you certainly don't lose your cool over a guy you hardly know—that is, until you get blindsided by him. For some reason, the guy who drives you crazy knows exactly when to pop into your life, lay it on real thick, and then wreak absolute havoc. Before you started hooking up with him, you were hardly a candidate for the rubber room, let alone someone who needed to see a therapist. But that was then, and now you're walking the fine line between a girl who's not afraid to go for what she wants and a girl who will stop at absolutely nothing to get it. FYI: The world doesn't need another Amy Fisher.

HIM, IN A NUTSHELL: As we already mentioned, your partner in the Joey Buttafuoco hookup should not be mistaken for an innocent victim—in fact, he could probably be considered a psycho himself. He's a natural charmer, good-looking, and has ADD when it comes to girls. He finds one, fawns all over her at his own convenience, and then moves on to his next prey before she even knows what hit her. He stays away from PDA because that would just be evidence that he is into a girl. Instead, he commits all of his offenses behind closed doors (for instance, he tells you that he really likes you in private, but then acts like he barely knows you in public). This way, when people ask him, "What in the world did you do to her to make her go psycho?," he can simply shrug and say, "I have no idea."

THE UPSIDE: You get to release some pent-up aggression.

> **EXAMPLE:** You listen to the Blondie song "One Way or Another" on repeat while doing your cardio kick tapes and get the best workout of your life.

BUYER BEWARE: You are so *that* girl.

> **EXAMPLE:** His friends don't even have to refer to you by name anymore—they just do the "cuckoo gesture" (twirling their pointer fingers in circles) and everybody knows who they mean.

IDENTIFYING FEATURES OF THE JOEY BUTTAFUOCO HOOKUP

1. **CIA SPECIAL AGENT PSYCHO:** You consider this hookup to be one great unsolved mystery and you're determined to crack the case. As part of your investigation, you conduct lots of undercover work, which includes driving very slowly past his house several times a day or calling him from any phone that's not yours (to throw him off your trail). Hopefully, all of this time and energy will yield an answer to the ultimate question: "Does he like me?"

2. **IT'S OPPOSITE DAY:** Quick psych lesson: There's this term known as "reaction formation." Basically, it means hiding how you really feel by doing something that is the exact opposite. This might explain why a Joey Buttafuoco situation drives you to act super friendly and cheerful around your hookup's potential female interests, when you secretly want to rip their heads off.

3. **GRIN AND BEAR IT:** Initially you try to hide the fact that this guy has a hold over you. When your friends gossip about him and another girl, you just smile through clenched teeth. However, you can only keep your game face for so long

before you bottom out.[10] The freakout won't be pretty, but acknowledging you have a problem is the first step on the road to recovery.

4. **JUSTIFY YOUR LOVE:** "But you don't *really* know him" becomes your favorite line. For some reason, everyone else can see that he's an asshole, but you're convinced that he just puts this alpha-male exterior up to protect himself from the cold, mean world (to you, he's really just a big teddy bear).

MORNING-AFTER ATTIRE: His favorite sweatshirt, which you plan on holding hostage until he kisses you like he means it

SIGNS THAT YOU'VE GONE A LITTLE TOO FAR

○ Whenever you walk into the room, you swear that you can hear someone faintly humming the theme to Jaws.

○ You create a new screen name so you can secretly monitor when he's online, when his ex-girlfriend is online, and when all of his friends are online.

○ You feel jealous when you see your best friend talking to him and start wondering if she's up to something.

---

[10] The bottoming out usually occurs after a few too many Long Island Iced Teas.

- You always wait around in the bar or at a party to be the last woman standing (and therefore, his only option).

- In an effort to make him jealous, you try to hook up with his friends.

- You buy him round after round of drinks, then sit back, nurse one Dos Equis, and watch your master plan unfold.

- You know more about him than his mother, his best friend, the government, and his doctor, combined.

- You honestly think that your friends, acquaintances, family, and hairstylist have him all wrong.

- You attempt to take up all of his favorite hobbies, which include fishing and car repair, in an effort to have more in common with him.

- You send his mother a card on her birthday signed "Love, your future daughter-in-law."

WHY IT ENDS: Your friends stage an intervention, during which they force you to come to terms with your temporary insanity. As part of your "treatment," they help you exorcise him from your life by torching his sweatshirt in your backyard.

HELL HATH NO FURY
GREAT PSYCHOTIC WOMEN
OF THE SILVER SCREEN

If you look back at your behavior during this hookup and feel a little embarrassed, don't fret. Check out these fabulously crazy ladies from the movies. You couldn't hold a candle to their insanity.

- Alicia Silverstone in *The Crush*: Lolita Psycho

- Cameron Diaz in *Vanilla Sky*: Road Ragin' Psycho

- Bridget Fonda in *Single White Female*: Your Freshman-Year-Roommate Psycho

- Drew Barrymore in *Poison Ivy*: ET Phone 911, There's a Crazy Bitch in Bed with Dad Psycho

- Erika Christensen in *Swimfan*: Wet and Wild Psycho

- Glenn Close in *Fatal Attraction*: Cheaters Never Win Psycho

- Kathy Bates in *Misery*: You'll Never Walk Out on Me Psycho

THE HIMBO
The Boy Toy Hookup

THE SCENARIO: A friend of a friend gets your name on the list at the brand-new, so-hot-right-now, one-word-name lounge (like "Lush" or "Coy"). After pushing to the front of the crowd, the headset-adorned doorman grants you and your plus-one access to the land of the beautiful people. While sipping a twelve-dollar mojito, you lock eyes with quite possibly the hottest guy you've ever seen, and holy shit, he's actually smiling at you. Before you can say "Jordan Catalano," he walks over and introduces himself. You're so blinded by his beauty that you can barely manage to tell him your name. He takes you to his friend's table in the VIP room, where the two of you spend the rest of the evening downing free drinks and having an amazingly deep conversation about absolutely nothing.

HIM, IN A NUTSHELL: Contrary to what you might think, you don't have to live somewhere like New York, Los Angeles, or Miami to encounter this pretty breed of boy (even though plenty of himbos flock to big cities in pursuit of fame and fortune). The himbo is devastatingly handsome, with sunny highlights and an even sunnier disposition (kind of like a golden retriever). In fact, he'd be abnormally friendly for a *regular* guy—let alone one blessed with flawless bone structure. Himbos are eternally in school, studying (part-time) to become something or other, but they make ends meet by pouring cocktails, deejaying parties, posing in front of the camera, or training clients at the gym (see "Let's Hear It for the Boy Toy" on page 151). They never seem to live in the same place for too long, and as a result, stay glued to their cell phones (which store no less than four hundred numbers). While he has enough intelligence to operate his state-of-the-art Nokia, it's safe to assume that the himbo is not the sharpest tool in the shed.

THE UPSIDE: He's just so damn beautiful that you can't believe you get to get with such a perfect male specimen.

> **EXAMPLE: Every time you kiss him you feel like you're in one of those Calvin Klein Eternity ads.**

BUYER BEWARE: Thanks to his chiseled everything, the amount of attention he receives tends to make you feel a little uncomfortable.

> **EXAMPLE: If you leave him alone at the bar for even a second, a couple of girls (and at least one guy) have already slipped him their numbers.**

IDENTIFYING FEATURES OF THE HIMBO HOOKUP

1. **BEAUTY AND THE BEAST COMPLEX:** The himbo has a better everything than you do (not counting IQ). This makes you start feeling a little insecure about the way you look compared to him. Come on. No amount of exfoliation could give you his smooth, glowing skin. Damn his genetics!

2. **SUGAR MOMMY:** The drinks are on you, the appetizers are on you, and the movie is on you. The himbo never has any cash on hand, so you end up footing the bill for everything. But honestly, with a face like that, how can you possibly hold a grudge against him?

3. DEAD AIR: Don't expect any deep conversation to come out of his pretty little mouth. In fact, keep it to the bare minimum: television (but never the news), movies (but only comedies), and working out (just stay away from big words like "anaerobic").

4. BIRDS OF A FEATHER: You'll never see him go anywhere without his posse of other himbos: There's J.D., the model from Texas who has done "some catalog work," J.C., the wannabe pop star with a dance single that's climbing to the top of the charts in Japan, and J.R., the aspiring actor who just got a big break playing "Male Nurse No. 1" on *The Bold and the Beautiful*.

MORNING-AFTER ATTIRE: He always sleeps at your place and ends up snagging one of your baby tees — which he looks hotter in than you ever could.

LET'S HEAR IT FOR THE BOY TOY
TYPES OF HIMBOS

Not all himbos are created equal. For instance, some like low weight and high reps, while others prefer high weight and low reps.

THE GREAT OUTDOORS HIMBO: He *loves* the wilderness—and can sleep in a tent for days and look like he stayed at the Four Seasons.

> **THINK:** The Brawny Paper Towel Man

MUSICIAN HIMBO: He always wants you to check out his next gig, wears leather pants, and thinks Billie Holiday is a man.

> **THINK:** Enrique Iglesias

MODEL HIMBO: He has no visible body hair, sports a belly ring, and hopes to become the next "face" of a man's fragrance line.

> **THINK:** Marcus Schenkenberg

ACTOR HIMBO: He constantly babbles about his "craft," auditions for nonspeaking roles, and tries to emulate the career of serious performers like Ashton Kutcher.

> **THINK:** Paul Walker

PERSONAL TRAINER HIMBO: He possesses a natural six-pack, always sports tight white tank tops and Adidas pants (the tearaway kind), and wears a do-rag to the gym.

> **THINK:** Eric Nies in *The Grind Workout*

BARTENDER HIMBO: So what if he doesn't know the difference between a Sidecar and a Manhattan? He looks sexy as hell trying to figure out how to make them.

> **THINK:** Tom Cruise in *Cocktail*

SPIRITUAL HIMBO: He recently discovered Buddhism, carries around a copy of the *Tao of Pooh* (which he has yet to finish), and meditates in his boxer briefs.

> **THINK:** Hansel (Owen Wilson's character in *Zoolander*)

WHY IT ENDS: He finally gets his big break and moves to Paris to do some runway shows. The next time you see him is during a segment on *Access Hollywood*, partying with P. Diddy in St. Tropez.

HE'S GOT GREAT PECS, BUT THAT DOESN'T NECESSARILY MAKE HIM A GRADE-A, 100 PERCENT USDA-APPROVED HIMBO

Himbos come and himbos go—often in the blink of an eye. It's just the nature of these pretty, jet-setting boys. Here's how to tell a real-deal himbo from just another pretty face.

HE MIGHT BE A HIMBO IF:

- He knows the circumference of his biceps.
- He was ever "discovered."
- He gets hit on by more guys than girls.
- He has that hot V-muscle on his hips.
- He makes most of his money in tips.
- He lived in another country and didn't learn a word of the language.

- He's six years into his undergrad program and still hasn't declared a major.

- He looks great in a white T-shirt.

- He never has to pay for anything.

- His workout consists of snowboarding, yet he still looks amazing.

- Most of his friends are "self-employed."

- He has a tasteful tattoo in a concealed (i.e., girly) spot, like his lower back or his stomach.

- He works Thursday through Saturday.

- He wears a knit skullcap year-round.

HE'S DEFINITELY NOT A HIMBO IF:

- He has a sense of irony.

- He can name the capital of the state
  he currently resides in.

- He reads the *Wall Street Journal*.

- He has a 401K.

- He has lived in the same place for three years
  (and doesn't plan on moving any time soon).

- He has a hairy chest.

- He votes.

- He has a gym membership (and rarely uses it).

- He golfs.

- He drives a sedan.

- He wakes up before noon (even on weekends).

- He books his vacations through a travel agent.

- He has to wait in line for anything.

- He wore braces and a retainer when he was a kid.

I THOUGHT WE HAD
SOMETHING SPECIAL
The Boy Who Wants More

THE SCENARIO: It starts out harmless enough. You come across
a decent guy with whom you share some decent conversation.
So you slip him your real phone number,[11] which he surprisingly
dials within forty-eight hours of meeting you. *Okay,* you think.
A little soon, but why not? It's not like you're going to marry him or
anything—plus, it's kind of refreshing. You meet him for drinks
and one thing leads to another and you hook up. This scenario
repeats itself a couple more times in the following weeks: He calls,
you join him for some cocktails, followed by a hookup. You're just
having a little fun. Guys do it all the time, don't they?

Well, you start feeling guilty when you sense that he wants a little
more intimacy out of this arrangement than you do. (Come on, he
called you at 2 A.M. on a Monday to talk about the death of Rusty, his
Irish setter.) So, rather than telling him straight out that you're not in
the market for a boyfriend, you break the Golden Hookup Rule[12] and

---

[11] You haven't been giving this out to every guy you "give your number" to,
have you?

[12] "Do not screw over others unless you don't mind being screwed over yourself."

simply stop returning his calls. You know it's an awful thing to do, but it probably means nothing to him too. Riiight . . .

After a few days of phone avoidance, you show up at work to find a voice mail from him (how did he get your office number, anyway?): "Hi. I miss you. I guess you've been really busy and that's why you haven't been returning my calls? Oh, and I can't live without you."

Guess he didn't get the hint.

HIM, IN A NUTSHELL: You should have known from the beginning that the Boy Who Wants More was going to be trouble. He has two distinct personalities: the charmer and the lovestruck lunatic. You initially get acquainted with the charmer. He showers you with compliments and hangs on every word you say; he uses flattery to reel you into his codependent world. When he casually mentions that he has "attachment issues," you just laugh it off.

The lovestruck lunatic, on the other hand, appears as soon as you think it's just a hookup. He's probably needy for attention or just fantastically nuts. No matter what his motivations are, he has a void that needs to be filled, and guess what? You'll do for now! He finds out your home phone number, work e-mail, and work extension and utilizes all three of them to tell you about the passion in his heart.

THE UPSIDE: All of his attention makes you feel really desirable.

> **EXAMPLE:** You accidentally let out a burp and he tells you that it's the cutest thing he's ever heard and you're the cutest girl he's ever seen.

BUYER BEWARE: He's way too emotional about everything in life, which makes you wonder what will happen when you stop hooking up with him.

> **EXAMPLE:** He punched through his bedroom wall when Clay Aiken lost on *American Idol*.

MORNING-AFTER ATTIRE: His favorite button-down (which, now that you've worn it, he'll never wash again)

IDENTIFYING FEATURES OF THE "I THOUGHT WE HAD SOMETHING SPECIAL" HOOKUP

1. **LOVE THE ONE YOU'RE WITH:** While you'd secretly like to believe that your gorgeous smile and amazing personality are driving him insane with passion, you know better: No sane guy would turn into a stalker after engaging in a couple of so-so make-out sessions with a girl: You just happened to be in the right place at the right time. You are not the first object of his obsession—oops, we mean *affection*—and definitely not the last.

2. **TOO MUCH INFORMATION:** You just met the guy and here he is, spilling the beans about his inadequacy issues and the collapse of his parents' marriage. Hello, why can't he talk about the unseasonably warm weather or what happened on *The Real World* last week? You love having deep conversations—when you actually know the person you're talking to.

3. **THE THRILL IS GONE:** We all like a challenge. Unfortunately, snagging the Boy Who Wants More is about as difficult as getting through a Danielle Steel novel. He makes himself way too available and vulnerable for his own good. (How could you ever be attracted to a guy who says, "I could get lost in your eyes" and actually means it?)

4. **PASSIVE-AGGRESSION:** As soon as his behavior turns weird, you attempt to phase him out. You stop returning his phone calls and delete his e-mails as soon as they pop up in your inbox. Unfortunately, this nonconfrontational approach only encourages him to take more drastic measures[13] to get your attention. Finally, after he calls your cell for the fifth time in one day without leaving a message, you reach your limit. You end up calling him and screaming into your phone, "Please leave me alone, you crazy bastard!"

---

[13] Meaning psychotic.

IS HE CRAZY IN LOVE OR CRAZY AS HELL?

CRAZY IN LOVE	CRAZY AS HELL
Sends flowers to your office	Sends Louie the Singing Gorilla to your office to perform "It Had to Be You"
Frequently checks your Friendster profile	Changes his Friendster profile so that it bears an eerie resemblance to yours (including listing *Clueless* and *Dirty Dancing* as his favorite movies)
Stares longingly into your eyes	Stares longingly into your bedroom window from your backyard

CRAZY IN LOVE	CRAZY AS HELL
Gets a little jealous when he sees you talking to your ex-boyfriend at the bar	Gets jealous when you talk to your best friend, mother, father, sister, that guy who works at Subway, etc.
Calls you up at night just to say hi	Calls you up at night just to breathe heavily into the phone
Says he likes spending time with you	Has done some time
Is into PDA	Is into public S&M
Asks your friends if you really like him	Hires a private investigator to find out if you really like him
Wants to jump into a serious relationship	Vows to jump off a bridge if you don't want a serious relationship
Wears his heart on his sleeve	Carves your name into his chest

HOW IT ENDS: The "I Thought We Had Something Special" hookup can end in so many exciting ways:

ENDING 1: The court grants you a restraining order.

ENDING 2: He goes away for a long, restful "vacation," where he can channel his emotions through finger painting.

ENDING 3: He gets a new obsession.

HOW TO MAKE HIM
SOMEONE ELSE'S PROBLEM

You realize that ignoring his phone calls, e-mails, text messages, and faxes doesn't work. Here's how to lose him without sending him completely over the edge.

- Tell him—with the straightest face possible— that you're gay.

- Make your two beefiest guy friends walk around with you all week and introduce them to everyone as your bodyguards. Hopefully, he'll get the hint.

- Send out a fake change of address and phone number mass e-mail to him. (Be sure to clue in all your friends that you're not actually moving.)

- Drop him off at the local Kabbalah or Scientology center.

- Pawn him off on your slightly psycho friend, who thought it was a "sweet gesture" when he parked outside your apartment at 4 A.M. and played "Every Breath You Take" on his car stereo until sunrise. The two of them can live together in chemically imbalanced bliss.

THE SNUFFLEUPAGUS
The Hookup You Deny but Everyone Else Knows Really Exists

THE SCENARIO: Once in a while we all do something we know is wrong for us, but for some reason we just can't exercise self-control.[14] That's the Snuffleupagus: the minute you meet him you've already thought of six hundred reasons why he's the *worst* possible guy for you. But for some reason you can't stop fantasizing about what it would be like to hook up with him. You feel repulsed, yet intrigued, and it's driving you absolutely crazy. Then one night you have a little too much to drink and end up getting it on with him. You *could* blame your lack of judgment on the alcohol, but you have this weird feeling that you actually had fun. So you hook up with him again—just to see, of course. And shit, you have such a good time with him that you're beginning to worry about having to hide this little affair from your friends. (Obviously, they would never understand how *you* could be with *him*.)

---

[14] For example, last year you wore a pair of leg warmers just because everyone said the eighties were back. Don't deny it.

164

HIM, IN A NUTSHELL: The Snuffleupagus is not your type. In fact, it'll be a cold day in hell before he's your type. Maybe he's too short, too simple, or even worse—he's a Republican. Whatever it is, it's definitely a deal-breaker for you, so hooking up with him would totally make you look like the biggest hypocrite in the world—or would it? You try to reason with yourself, but it's just no use; you can't get him out of your head. And once you actually take the plunge, you start sympathizing with heroin addicts because you now understand the meaning of addiction. It might not even be that he's so amazing between the sheets; it could be that he makes you laugh or he makes you feel like a goddess, but you just can't deny (at least to yourself, since there is no way you are telling anyone) that he is one of the best hookups you've ever had—by far. And while you continue to secretly rendezvous with him, you never let yourself get too attached. He's just your dirty little secret until Mr. Right comes along.

THE UPSIDE: Since you're refraining from giving your friends all the dirty details, this hookup is completely untainted by their opinions and comments (thank God).

> **EXAMPLE:** The only advice you get is from fortune cookies and your Magic 8 ball.

BUYER BEWARE: You could be passing up someone really cool.

> **EXAMPLE:** **He's the only other person you know who remembers all the original *DeGrassi Junior High* episodes.**

IDENTIFYING FEATURES OF THE SNUFFLEUPAGUS HOOKUP

1. **ACCIDENTALLY ON PURPOSE:** You swore that he was a one-time mistake. But one fateful Friday night, you went out, got ridiculously drunk, and just happened to bump into him at the bar. What were the odds? After that point in the evening, things get really hazy. . . . In reality, you drank two beers, used your CSI investigative skills to scope out his location, and remember everything in vivid detail, but your friends never need to know that, do they?

2. **TELLING TALL TALES:** In an effort to keep your secret, your little half-truths morph into fantastic lies. Suddenly you are capable of time travel, being in two places at once, and working oodles of overtime at the office. If your friends were smart, they would enjoy shooting holes in your story and watching you squirm.

3. **YIN AND YANG:** Your life splits into two distinct halves: day and night. In the daylight, you can't believe that you ever hooked up with him. But as soon as the sun sets and the drinks start flowing, that little voice in your head whispers, "Go ahead. Call him up. No one will ever know."

4. **AN ADMISSION OF GUILT, TWO YEARS TOO LATE:** Maybe you're reliving your junior high days and playing a game of Never Have I Ever. For a giggle, your best friend says, "Never have I ever made out with [insert the name of your Snuffleupagus hookup here]." In a moment of absolute confession, you blush and admit that—ohmygod—you have!!!! Since they don't have the heart to let you in on your not-so-secret little secret, your friends feign surprise and suppress their true sentiment, which is: "No shit, Sherlock."

THE SIX BEST WAYS
TO COVER YOUR TRACKS

Don't make the mistake of slipping up and telling unbelievable tales in an effort to keep your Snuffy a secret. These white lies are so slick, even Nancy Drew couldn't figure out what you've been up to.

1. **ACQUIRE AN ACCOMPLICE:** You need to find a neutral party who your friends don't know. This person can serve as an alibi whenever you need one. Coworkers make a good choice because they are removed from your social scene, but they're not so random that your friends might get suspicious when you're hanging out with Kate from payroll every Friday night.

2. **GIVE HIM A PSEUDONYM:** You wouldn't be dumb enough to program his number in your cell under his real name, right? Of course you would. To prevent your pals from seeing Snuffy's name pop up on the screen, put him in your phone as something completely random. We recommend the name of a gay male friend, if you have one. That should throw everyone off the track.

3. **THINK FAST:** You need to have answers ready for a multitude of questions. For example: Your best friend spies a hickey on your neck and demands to know who gave it to

you. You should quickly, yet breezily, answer with: "There was a curling iron incident and, well, things got ugly."

4. **HIT THE BOOKS:** If you're in college, then the library is the safest place for the two of you to make out for hours without being caught by anyone you know.

5. **CREATE A DISTRACTION:** Take a cue from any amateur magician and utilize the principle of distraction: Make your friends focus all their attention on one thing so they don't even realize what's happening in front of their noses. Here's how it works: Fake having a crush on a guy who is totally out of your league and constantly obsess about him to your friends. Make the bold declaration that he's the only man for you and that you couldn't possibly even think of touching any other guy.

6. **USE REVERSE-REVERSE PSYCHOLOGY (I.E., PSYCHOLOGY):** Any moron would think it's a good idea to talk shit about their Snuffy whenever his name comes up in conversation, foolishly thinking that their friends would be duped by a few low blows. The better option is to remain completely poker-faced at just the mention of his name. Always remember: Never let 'em see you sweat.

MORNING-AFTER ATTIRE: What morning-after attire? You stayed in last night and watched HBO (wink, wink).

WHY IT ENDS: Without warning, he simply gets over you and moves on to someone else. You object: Weren't you supposed to get rid of him? After a few jealous attempts to rekindle your secret affair, you give up. Of course, now you actually find him attractive and kick yourself for letting a good one get away.

CUT HIM SOME SLACK

Before you write off your undercover hookup because he's so not right for you, remember that you've been wrong about things in the past. Don't believe us? Okay. Here's a little reminder. You used to think:

- Boys had cooties.
- No one in his right mind would make a sequel to *Scooby Doo*.
- High school was the best time of your life.
- A Brazilian WHAT?!

- Parents just don't understand.

- Britney was the next Madonna.

- Fluorescent pink was the new black.

- Thirty was way old.

- Beer before liquor, never been sicker. Liquor before beer, in the clear.

- Your ex really did want to stay friends.

- Your pet goldfish was doing the backfloat.

- Your parents were just wrestling.

- Fat-free cookies wouldn't make you fat.

- George Michael was straight.

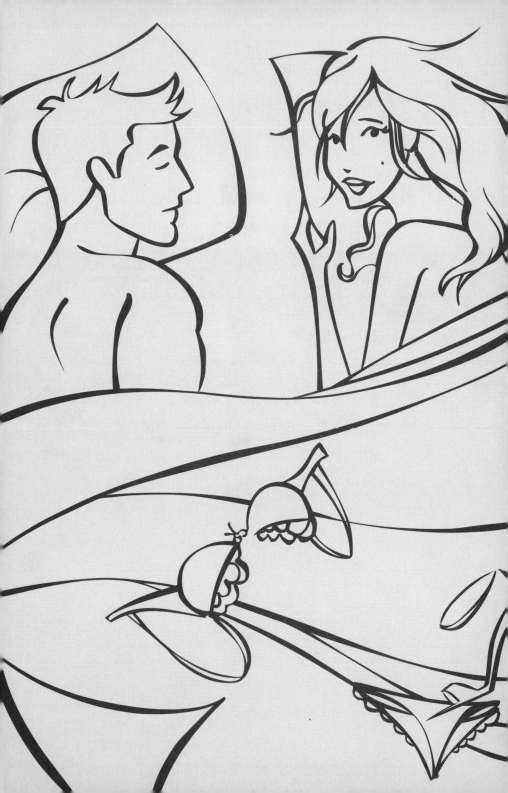

PART III

THE MORNING AFTER

What Happens When the Buzz Wears Off

RISE AND SHINE
Who the Hell Are You and What Are You Doing on My Side of the Bed?

Question: What do Crystal Pepsi, Nader 2004, and spiral perms all have in common? Answer: They seemed like a good idea at the time. Think of hooking up in the same way: In the heat of the moment, it's all fun and games. But after the haze of cigarette smoke clears and your buzz is replaced by a throbbing headache, things can get a little awkward. And nothing, um, *illuminates* this difference between hookup and post-booty more than the bright sun shining in on your unwashed face on a Sunday morning. Yikes.

Don't get us wrong. We're not saying that all hookups turn into horror as soon as the sun rises in the east (or that hookups even need to span into the morning). It's just that many things, like Barbara Walters and our asses in the dressing room mirror at Macy's, look better in soft lighting.

Night sets the scene for most hookups. It's a parallel universe where cocktails, hormones, and Top 40 hip-hop supersede reason, judgment, and inhibitions—kind of like the Twilight Zone with an open tab.[15]

Unfortunately, you can't live in that blissful state forever. A Saturday night is a lot like school recess: Just when the action starts to heat up, the playground aide blows the whistle and forces everyone back into their classrooms. In the grown-up world, the sunrise replaces the playground aide, and the classroom is the morning after.

The dawn of a new day reminds us that a world exists outside the protective bubble of cocktails and moonlight—and what a cruel, cruel world it can be, and is that really a J.Lo poster hanging on his bedroom wall? Yes. Yes it is. The morning after is one tough cookie—it exposes things you really didn't want to see, and can make for some awkward situations.

---

[15] For example, when's the last time you drank four shots of Southern Comfort and danced on the bar to "Sweet Home Alabama" during your lunch break? Yeah, that's what we thought.

Let's face it, the last thing you want to do when you wake up next to some guy you just hooked up with is actually have a conversation with him. All you want in the world is to take a shower and call your friends to rehash last night's details. (After the hangover has left your body, you can think about what steps you'd like to take in your hookup situation.)

If you're at his place, then you need to get home (see "Not the Time to Stop for a Danish and Coffee: The Walk of Shame Rears Its Uncombed Head" on page 179). On the other hand, if he's snoring away in your bed, this leaves you in quite a bind. You want him to leave, but you don't know how to show him the door without coming off as a terrible, heinous person. What's a girl to do in this situation? Before we go any further, consider this injustice: Often, when you actually like a guy and want him to stay so that last night's hookup session might continue into the morning, he wakes up at 8 A.M. and makes some awful excuse as to why he needs to leave right away.[16] On the other hand, if the guy's more irritating than poison ivy, he seems to have no problem making himself right at home.[17] It's like Confucius says: *"When you like boy he not stay, when you no like boy he stay all day."* And when it comes to the guy who just won't leave, a simple, "Wow! I didn't

---

[16] "Um, I have a lot of shit I need to do."

[17] And did he use your toothbrush? Ewww.

realize what time it is, I need to get up and make that early pilates class" isn't going to get him out. Here are a few more aggressive things you can say that will not only have him racing out the door, but will also guarantee he never hogs your covers again.

BYE BYE BYE
WHAT TO SAY TO SEND HIM ON HIS WAY

- I love you.

- I have to pick up my husband at the airport in an hour. Wanna come with?

- I have a brunch date with my parole officer.

- Where do you see this going?

- Do you think I'm fat?

- I have diarrhea.

- My kids are going to love you!

- So, do you wanna go get skim lattes and see [insert title of latest chick flick here]?

- Last one to the free clinic is a rotten egg!

- That will be one hundred dollars.

- It's not me, it's you.

NOT THE TIME TO STOP FOR A DANISH AND COFFEE
The Walk of Shame Rears Its Uncombed Head

The Merriam-Webster Dictionary defines the "walk of shame" as, um, absolutely nothing. They haven't caught up with the times yet.[18] The rest of us know that the walk of shame means having to walk home from someone else's residence after a hookup, and it is usually identifiable by disheveled hair, smudged mascara, and an outfit that just doesn't look right at 10 A.M. on a Sunday.

---

[18] But they do have entries for "brewski," "def," and "phat." Go figure.

THIS IS NO WALK IN THE PARK

So why is the walk of shame such a universal trauma? Well, it's all fun and games when you and a guy drunkenly stumble, arm-in-arm, back to his place in the middle of the night to "watch a movie." But it's a totally different story when you have to walk down that same road the next morning on your way home, sporting a bustier and one shoe. Here are a few more reasons why this journey is more sobering than a cup of black coffee and an ice-cold shower.

YOU'VE BEEN FOUND GUILTY

The night before, you were able to keep that evil little voice (also known as your conscience) at bay. But as the light of day beats down on your partied-out body, you can't help but think, *Should I have done that?* In this age of so-called sexual liberation, double standards are alive and kicking. For example: Cool guys get their rocks off, good girls hold out for a rock. Or what about this one: Ladies should go out, have fun, and break the rules—just as long as no one ever finds out about it. These conflicting social messages could help contribute to your guilt factor (or maybe you just shouldn't have hooked up with your friend's boyfriend, you homewrecker).

YOU'RE NOT LEAVING THE HOUSE LOOKING LIKE THAT, YOUNG LADY!

An inverse relationship exists between the severity of your walk of shame and the amount of clothing you wore out the night before: the skimpier the outfit, the higher the trauma factor. That's because strolling down the street in evening apparel (we're not talking jeans and a T-shirt here) before you've even had breakfast lets everyone know that you slept somewhere other than your own bed last night. Everywhere from college campuses to city blocks, the most popular walk of shame ensemble usually involves some kind of boobalicious top, a skintight pair of jeans (or an ass-cheek-exposing miniskirt), open-toed shoes, and a teeny-tiny purse that barely fits a tampon. (This outfit makes appearances year-round—even in the dead of winter.) Don't worry too much if you get caught in a tube top or some barely there schoolgirl number at 9 A.M.: While these looks are definitely better suited for partying than for scarfing down brunch, they certainly won't elicit anything more than a few stares (okay, and the occasional proposition). If anyone really hassles you, simply say that you're doing undercover work for the FBI and will bust a cap in their ass if they get any closer.

WHO ARE THE PEOPLE IN *HIS* NEIGHBORHOOD?

You know how it goes when you have a klutzy moment: You're walking down the street in your platform sandals and out of nowhere, you bite it on the pavement. What's your first reaction? That's right: You look around in a panic to see if anyone saw you trip over your own feet. Well, it's the same thing with the walk of shame—the witnesses are what make this moment so freaking mortifying. It's bad enough when you think a random stranger is casting confused glances in your direction, but it's the absolute worst when you run into someone you know." Now, you can handle this sticky situation in one of two ways: You can totally acknowledge that person like it's just a typical morning and act as if you're not wearing a Dallas Cowgirls cheerleading uniform, or you can keep your head down and pretend that you don't see Mr. Barrett, the man who taught you how to do long division.

OH, THE PLACES YOU WILL GO!

It's one thing if you're able to stumble back into your apartment after an endless night, pry your contacts out of your eyes, splash some warm water on your face, grunt at your roommate, and

---

" Double the freak-out factor when that person happens to be any of the following: a coworker, your boss, your ex-boyfriend, your boyfriend, a friend of a friend, or your eighth-grade math teacher.

retreat to your bed for the rest of the day. It's a whole new problem, though, if you have to take your walk of shame directly to your office or to your grandfather's eightieth birthday party. In this case, not only do you have to deal with people, but you also feel like absolute shit (and run the risk of having to toss your cookies during a meeting with your boss).

YOU'RE STILL FEELING THE BUZZ

In the highly unlikely case that you had one too many appletinis the night before (because we all know that "just one drink" means having three, "going for drinks" means five, and "going out drinking" equals recreating the night you turned twenty-one), there's a good chance that alcohol is still running through your bloodstream like wild horses. As a result, you feel the tail end of drunkenness—the prelude to a hangover (think dizziness, an impending headache, and racing, uncontrollable thoughts clamoring around in your brain). Add to the mix some sleep deprivation and moderate dehydration, and you've guaranteed that your mind and reflexes are as sharp as a lump of Play-Doh. No wonder you think everyone's staring at you. You just need to get some shut-eye, girl. We swear, the paperboy doesn't know that you got some last night.

ONE, SINGULAR SENSATION

Part of what makes the walk of shame so shameful is that you have to do it all by your lonesome. Just imagine how fun it would be if you and your friend met up on the corner and escorted each other home. You could swap details about your respective evenings and maybe even stop to grab some pancakes (and, of course, coffee—lots of coffee). The hidden bonus of threesomes: If you and the girl hit it off, then you have a buddy to share the walk home with the next morning.

HOW TO TAKE THE SHAME OUT OF YOUR WALK

Since it's safe to assume that you're not traveling with some kind of overnight bag, complete with a toiletry case and a change of clothes, you're going to have to improvise (think *MacGyver* meets Martha Stewart).

To ease your walk-of-shame anxieties, here are ten ways to make the long and winding road from his door to yours a little less stressful. These tips also work if you have to meet up with friends or family and you don't have a chance to stop home first.

1. **REMOVE YOUR EYE MAKEUP BEFORE YOU GO TO BED.** Oh, who are we kidding—you probably passed out mid–makeout session, so in that case you should take off your mascara and liner right before you leave his place in the morning. Raccoon eyes are a surefire sign of a night of commitment-free fun. And since it's unlikely that he'll have Clinique Gentle Eye Makeup Remover at his place (if he does, he's either a drag queen or he has a girlfriend), locate a jar of Vaseline, ignore the fact that he owns a large jar of Vaseline, and use a dab to tissue off your eye makeup.

2. **TIE YOUR HAIR BACK.** You can always tell how hot the hookup was by how messed up your hair looks in the morning. Even if it was on the PG side, it's still possible to wake up with dreadlocks. If you're not lucky enough to have a hair elastic around your wrist or a spare in your purse, look around his place for a rubber band. None to be found? Take the metal twist-tie off his bread and use it to pull your hair off your face.[20]

---

[20] Ever wonder why so many girls dress up as French maids for costume parties? It's because the garter belt doubles as a scrunchie the next morning.

3. **LOSE THE COSTUME ACCESSORIES.** As we mentioned earlier, the best part of going to a costume party is having an excuse to dress in a really slutty outfit, complete with really slutty accessories like a boa, bunny ears, and fishnet stockings. Get rid of them *before* leaving his place. As sad as it may be to leave your beloved props on the floor of his room, just know that if you step out into daylight wearing any of the aforementioned things, you'll run the risk of looking like a stripper who just got off work.

4. **HIDE YOUR EYES.** Bloodshot eyes let the world know that not only were you out really late the night before, but you were probably doing things during the night other than sleeping. Fake a full night of sin-free sleep by locating eyedrops in his bathroom—or better yet, just steal one of his baseball caps and pull it down really low.

5. **CURE YOUR STINKY BREATH.** A combination of alcohol, cigarettes, and not brushing your teeth before you crash can make your breath smell beyond offensive. Some girls stuff a toothbrush in their purse when they think they'll be making

a night of it with their hookup, but we think that's a little presumptuous. Instead, swish cold water around in your mouth, then use the old finger and toothpaste trick to get your breath in decent shape.

6. **RAID HIS CLOSET.** When the weather starts heating up, most girls happily head out for the night in skimpier ensembles, leaving their jackets and cardigans in the closet. The problem is that you have nothing to cover you up while you walk home the next morning. So instead of parading through the streets in a postage-stamp-size skirt, borrow one of his button-down shirts. Tie it around your waist so the whole world doesn't have to see your ass.

7. **DISTRACT YOURSELF.** As soon as you leave his place, whip out your cell and dial one of your friends who won't kill you for waking her up before noon. Or better yet, take this opportunity to call your grandma (chances are, she won't think anything of the fact that you're calling from your cell phone at 8:20 A.M. on a Saturday). The point is to do something that'll take your attention away from the walk, while making you look too busy to care that your bra is stuffed inside your pocketbook.

8. **DON'T STOP FOR COFFEE.** As tempting as it may be to just run into the local Starbucks to grab a much-needed venti house blend, you'll inevitably regret this decision when you're forced to wait in line between your rabbi and your best friend's mom.

9. **MAKE AN EARLY GETAWAY.** It's always ideal to leave his place before 9 A.M., since the only people out and about around that time are usually joggers (and they usually move too fast to even notice you).

10. **HAVE HIM SLEEP AT YOUR PLACE.** DUH!

POP QUIZ
How Shameful Was Your Walk of Shame?

There is the garden-variety walk of shame, and then there is the supreme stumble, the incredible journey from what's-his-name's back to the comfort and safety of your own bed. Take the quiz on the following pages to see just how bad your walk of shame was.

1. In terms of length, my walk was:

   a. right around the block.

   b. less than a mile.

   c. equivalent to the "Walk for Hunger" that I did back in eighth grade.

2. Physical markings from the night before:

   a. hand stamp from the club

   b. hickey

   c. tattoo of his name on my ass

3. Where was my bra?

   a. I was wearing it.

   b. It was in my purse.

   c. It's still hanging over the bar.

4. During my journey home, I bumped into:

a. my physics lab partner.

b. a telephone pole.

c. my boyfriend.

5. My makeup resembled:

a. Courtney Love, pre-makeover.

b. Courtney Love, post-makeover.

c. Courtney Love, post-post makeover.

6. The Aerosmith song that best captured the atmosphere/mood of my walk home:

a. "Sweet Emotion"

b. "Living on the Edge"

c. "Dude Looks Like a Lady"

7. The weather was:

    a. partly sunny and mild.

    b. partly cloudy, 30 percent chance of showers.

    c. hurricane season.

8. On my feet were:

    a. flats.

    b. strappy sandals.

    c. one strappy sandal (never did find out what
    happened to the left shoe . . .).

9. Hangover status:

    a. nothing a strong cup of coffee couldn't cure

    b. nothing an omelette, home fries, and a Bloody
    Mary couldn't cure

    c. nothing five hours spent praying to the
    porcelain gods couldn't cure

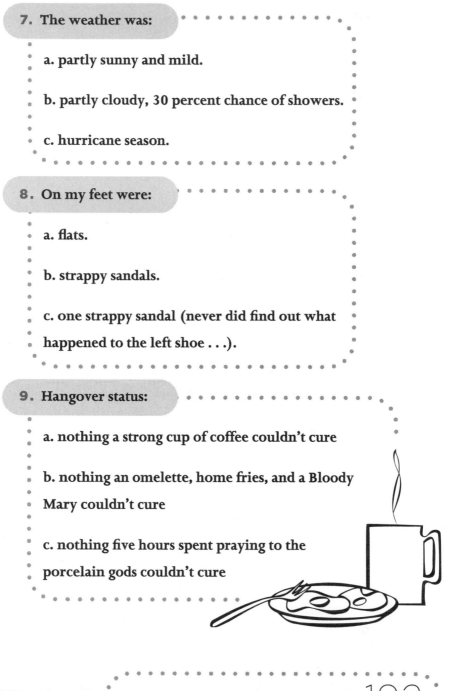

10. How well did I function the rest of the day?

  a. At about 90 percent. I could have operated heavy machinery if I had to.

  b. So-so. I was able to watch the entire first season of *Friends* on DVD without dozing off.

  c. Not so good. I fell asleep on the toilet—twice.

ANSWER KEY

If you answered mostly "a"s, then your walk was a "Walk in the Park": So, let's get this straight: You walked home in beautiful weather, wearing Aerosoles and a big smile on your face? Oh, boo-hoo. Life's tough, isn't it? Your walk of shame really sounds no different than taking a little stroll around the neighborhood on a sunny spring morning. Did you at least trip and fall over the curb?

If you answered mostly "b"s, then your walk was a "Semi-Embarrassing Saunter": Yikes, seems like you had a rough night, party girl. But fear not: I'm sure most people didn't even notice the fact that you were wearing a miniskirt, a tiara, and a hooded sweatshirt. Okay, maybe that little old lady who works at the convenience store on your corner did a double take when you stopped in to buy a bottle of water, but whatever.

If you answered mostly "c"s, then your walk was a "Death March": Good God, girl. When you walked down the street, mothers shielded their sons' eyes, fathers warned their daughters never to turn out like "that girl," and for a moment, it seemed like there was a total eclipse of the sun. Okay, so maybe that's a bit of an exaggeration (the part about the sun, at least), but you just gotta watch your step and make sure you don't end up in a ditch somewhere— and save your fishnets and knee-high boots for a midnight showing of The Rocky Horror Picture Show.

DIAL "D" FOR DRAMA
Pick Up the Phone and Call, Asshole

Unfortunately, the walk of shame is probably not the only post-hookup hurdle you'll have to deal with. Don't believe us? All righty. Take a good long look at your cell phone—that's right, your cute little flip phone, your connection to the outside world. Looks pretty unassuming, doesn't it? Now, why is it that as soon as you give a guy you hooked up with your digits, your pink Nokia morphs into an evil instrument capable of making a perfectly rational girl like you plead temporary insanity? There's only one explanation: Chalk it up to the complexities of post-hookup telecommunications.

No matter what type of hookup you have had—Best Bud Tryst, Putting in Overtime, Pass the Sippy Cup, et cetera—there will always be a certain amount of anxiety and anticipation surrounding that initial phone conversation. Will he ever call? How long will it take before he calls? What could we possibly talk about? Is he the one who keeps calling up in the middle of the night and breathing heavily into the receiver?

Before you scream, "What year is this—1958?! I don't sit home waiting for the phone to ring," don't worry, we couldn't agree more. Of course you don't sit home waiting for a guy to dial you up, because we now have an invention known as a *mobile phone*. "Mobile" means you can take your phone everywhere you go and annoy the shit out of all your friends when you check your voice mail every five minutes and whine, "Why hasn't he called yet?"

In all seriousness, there's no reason why you can't grab hold of the reins and give your new guy friend a call. Go ahead,

Ms. Twenty-First-Century Woman, put your money where your mouth is and call him first. We're not stopping you. And while you're at it, can you change our flat tire? There's a spare in the trunk.

For the rest of you girls who've ever been baffled by the phone games guys play, let's take a closer look at the phenomenon scientifically known as "pre-call anxiety." We're under the assumption here that you want him to be the first one to call.[21]

THE RULES OF THE TELEPHONE GAME

Logically, it seems that if you meet a cute boy while you're out one night, you smooch said boy, and he asks for your number, it should be a no-brainer that he'd call. Riiight. If only it were as simple as that. Now this may come as a shocking surprise, but just because a guy gets your digits, it doesn't automatically mean he's going to call. In fact, as most girls will tell you, a lot of times you never hear from him again. In that case it's safe to assume that he's been in a terrible accident and was found lying in a ditch somewhere, clutching your number in one hand and his cell phone in the other.

---

[21] We're assuming that you want a repeat performance with your hookup. If you'd rather go back to your natural hair color than ever see his face again, we suggest you change your phone number—or better yet, move to a commune in New Mexico.

The general rule of thumb when it comes to guys and rules of phone conduct was best summed up in the classic movie *Swingers*. In one particular scene, a group of guy friends debate about how long a self-respecting man should wait before calling a girl he just met or hooked up with. After a rather lengthy discussion, they tentatively decide that two days is the "industry standard." So that means if the hookup happens on Saturday night, you should pretty much expect a call on Monday night. But here's the ironic part: If a guy actually called on Monday night, most girls would complain that it was too soon and that he was stepping into stalker territory, in which case, ladies, can we please cut the guy some slack? That's why Tuesday night usually seems golden—it's not so soon after the encounter that he appears trigger-happy, but not too late in the week that it seems like he's merely flipping through his little black book in an attempt to secure a piece of ass for Saturday night.[22]

Of course, when he calls you also depends on how he got your digits in the first place (and we're assuming that you didn't send them to him telepathically). Things can get very complicated when numbers exchange hands. To help sort through this mess, let's take a look at the three main ways he gets your number and how each of these ways affects the rules of the telephone game.

---

[22] As if this weren't complicated enough, all rules go out the window during football season, since he'll probably be too busy sitting on the couch with one hand on the remote and the other hand down his pants to call you up in a timely fashion.

SCENARIO 1: YOU GIVE HIM YOUR BUSINESS CARD

Initially, giving a guy your business card seems like a good idea. After all, it provides him with the correct spelling of your first and last name (with your middle initial thrown in for good measure), your employer, your very important position within the company (they couldn't function without their senior executive assistant to the vice president), your work address, your work extension, your fax number, and your e-mail. However, there's something slightly impersonal about giving a boy you just made out with (or want to make out with) your business card. In addition, you have to realize that while it might seem savvy to give him a preprinted piece of paper that contains more than one way to get in touch with you, how likely is it that he's going to have the patience (and burning desire) to make it all the way through your company's automated voice mail system? You didn't think he was going to send you a "hey, what's up?" fax, did you? This leaves your e-mail address. While e-mail definitely serves as an efficient and acceptable form of communication in the world of hooking up, it's not exactly ideal. Boys aren't as on top of things as us girls, and it could be weeks before he stops writing you semi-flirty yet completely vague e-mails and actually calls you on the phone.

SCENARIO 2: YOU CONDUCT AN IN-THE-BAR CELL PHONE NUMBER EXCHANGE

If you're the type of girl who likes to assume that a guy accidentally lost your number and has spent several sleepless nights desperately ransacking his apartment trying to locate it, then this method is probably your best bet. Here's how it works: When he finally works up the nerve to ask for your number at the end of the night, instead of yelling it out over the blare of "You Shook Me All Night Long," grab his phone and dial your phone from his. This way, not only will he have your correct number, but you will have his (without even having to ask for it).

While this approach seems much more effective than scrawling your number on a grocery store receipt/napkin/matchbook cover/exposed patch of skin on his body, there are a couple of downsides to this hi-tech number exchange. First of all, his cell phone may hold only a limited amount of just-dialed digits in its memory before it pushes your precious number off into digital oblivion. (And do you really think he's going to wait until next month's itemized Verizon bill to hunt down the number of the cute girl from the bar who, for all he knows, could be married by now?) Another issue with the in-the-bar cell phone exchange is the

JACK
212-555-5656

fact that now you also have his number. So what are you going to do about it? This is a lot like when your parents gave you a Visa card in case of "emergencies": You have the power to never use it, to charge the occasional week's worth of groceries, or to go buck wild and max it out at Victoria's Secret.

SCENARIO 3: HE GETS YOUR NUMBER FROM A THIRD PARTY

There's nothing worse than spending an entire night smooching a cute boy who, for whatever reason (let's just say he's a complete moron), doesn't ask for your number. Well, all hope isn't lost, since it's entirely possible that he'll wake up the next morning and realize how stupid he was for not getting your digits. In that case, he might try to score them from a mutual friend. The odds of his succeeding in his mission are good if you were at a party in which you both had a direct link to the host or hostess (none of this six degrees of separation bullshit—we're talking *direct links*). And the rules clearly state that the friend who gives him your number is to immediately contact you and replay the conversation they had, word for word, so you can analyze it. (*"So wait—did he say I was 'cute' or I was 'hot'?"*) The only problem with this situation is that there are heightened expectations—now you *expect* him to call. How annoying is it if you find out that he hunted down your number and never used it? In the case of this unfortunate incident, you've just got to face the facts: He's finally coming to terms with his homosexuality. But look on the bright side. He'll probably call you up to go shoe shopping.

A FEW WORDS ABOUT DRUNK DIALING

It would be a total travesty to discuss hookup telecommunications without mentioning drunk dialing. To sum it up, drunk dialing is what happens when you have too many cocktails and no security code on your cell phone. It's deceiving, addictive, and often embarrassing. And that's because nine times out of ten you can't remember what the hell you rambled on about when you left him not one, not two, but three voice mails. On the flip side, when a guy drunk dials you, keep in mind that a phone call at 1:30 on a Saturday morning does not mean the same thing as that same guy actually making a sober phone call to you at 1:30 in the afternoon. (For more about this phenomenon, see "Q&A Session: Call Quandaries" on page 204.)

HONESTY IS THE BEST POLICY

What does all this in-depth analysis about something as seemingly benign as a phone teach us about hooking up? Well, for one thing, as long as there are guys and girls, there will always be lots of drama centered around the fact that he hasn't called. So the next time one of your friends whines, "When do you think he's going to call me?," do her a favor and don't feed her the same load of crap that girls have been saying to one another since the phone was invented.[23] Instead, look her straight in the eye and say, "My theory is that if a guy really likes you, he'll call. And if he doesn't like you, he may still call, but only if he is really drunk and horny." It might not be what she wants to hear, but it's the truth.

---

[23] "Don't worry, I'm sure the minute you stop thinking about it he'll call you."

Q&A SESSION
Call Quandaries

Q: I met a great guy and he finally called—on a Friday night at 12:50 A.M. And he was obviously slurring. Does he like me?

A: Well, that really depends on his location when he dialed your number. Does he live in California and you reside in New York, which would mean that he actually called you at the respectable hour of 9:50 P.M. Pacific Standard Time? Also, does he have some sort of speech impediment that would account for the difficulties he encountered while trying to carry on a conversation? If you answered "no" to either of these questions, then this sounds like a textbook case of drunk dialing—the cornerstone of hookup communications. If this happens again, then "Does he like me?" is not the appropriate question to be asking yourself. Instead, you should ponder, "Does he like me right now?" The answer will always be, "Yes, yes he does."

Q: I hooked up with this guy and we exchanged phone numbers. He called me a couple of days later and left a message on my voice mail. I promptly returned his call and left a message on his voice mail. It's been a week and I haven't heard back from him yet. What's the deal with that?

A: There's nothing more frustrating than playing a game of phone tag. It makes you think irrational thoughts when there's probably a very simple explanation as to why the other person didn't return your phone call. In this case, your guy is probably on vacation with his girlfriend in Barbados for the week and will return your call as soon as he gets back into the country.

Q: Help! What kinds of things should I talk about during my first phone conversation with him?

A: Appropriate topics of discussion for that initial phone call might include your job, the weather, reality TV, sports, vacation spots, how drunk you got last night, and what music you're currently listening to. Things you should never mention include past relationships, your current "medication vacation," the fact that you saw *The Passion of the Christ* twelve times in the movie theater, your biological clock, and what music the voices in your head are currently listening to.

Q: If I don't even like the guy, then why do I get upset when he doesn't call?

A: If you're a fan of clichés, then the correct way to answer this question is: "Because you always want what you can't have." See, in every hookup there is a rejecter and a rejectee. Since you didn't like this guy, you automatically assumed the role of the rejecter, which was your first mistake. In order to fulfill his position as the rejectee, he should call you a few times before he finally throws in the towel, heartbroken that you didn't second that emotion. But by not calling you, he actually turned the tables and left you in the undesirable position of being the rejectee. Just don't confuse being annoyed at him with actually liking him, because then you might end up doing something crazy like calling him.

Q: What does a guy think of a girl who calls him first? I don't want to seem desperate.

A: Relax. He'll think you're mighty cool—unless you call every hour on the hour or leave kissy sounds on his voice mail.

HE CALLED, NOW WHAT?
Going for a Repeat Performance

There you were, just hanging out at your apartment on a Wednesday night, lounging in your sweats and not even thinking about whether or not you were ever going to talk to him again. (That's why your cell phone was just resting comfortably in your dominant hand.) Then, all of a sudden, "Riiiiiiing!" False alarm—it's just your best friend calling at the commercial break to discuss the performances so far on *American Idol*.

As soon as the show comes back on your TV screen, you hear the beep of your call waiting and ohmygod you don't recognize the number. "I gotta go!" you yell to your friend and cut her off mid–good-bye, switching over into calm, cool, collected mode. An hour and a half later you're lying blissfully in your bed, mentally replaying the conversation you just had with him. You're positive that it went really well. You covered everything from favorite foods (*"Oh my god, you like sushi? That's soooo funny because I love sushi!"*) to what sport he played in high school (*"Wow, so you were the goalie? Isn't that like a really important position?"*) And the best part is that he asked you for plans. Now here's where things get tricky: If he says that you should try to meet up "over the weekend at a bar or something," then it's clearly in the jurisdiction of a hookup. On the other hand, if he asks you to meet up for drinks, then it could be a date—or is it? To find out exactly what type of outing he has in mind, you have to consider some key factors.

IS IT A HOOKUP OR A DATE?

- If he uses the words "stop by" or "meet up," it's definitely a hookup.

- If he says, "I'll pick you up at 8 o'clock," it's a date.

- If you can't hear a word he's saying over the beat of the music (and couldn't care less), it's a hookup.

- If he asks to see a wine list, it's definitely a date.

- If most of your quality time is spent in a bar, it's a hookup.

- If you feel obligated to laugh at all his lame jokes, it's definitely a date.

- If he asks, "What kind of shot do you want—So-Co or Jack?", it's definitely a hookup.

- If he says "we" in reference to his friends and him rather than you and him, it's a hookup.

- If he puts his hand on your thigh as soon as you see him, it's definitely a hookup.

- If you get tipsy together during dinner, it's a date.

- If you have to get mind-numbingly intoxicated before seeing him, it's a hookup.

- If one of you pays the check at the end of the evening, it's a date.

- If one of you closes the tab at the end of the evening, it's a hookup.

- If you can't tell your mother about it, it's definitely a hookup.

NONRELATIONSHIP LIMBO
Entering the What-the-Hell-Are-We Phase

Hookups come and hookups go. Sometimes they mysteriously disappear (like socks in a dryer), and other times things gets ugly and you vow to swear off guys forever (or at least until the next weekend). Still, there remain a few intriguing occasions when a hookup takes a more sobering direction. Rather than plodding along as a drunken grope fest, you and your Saturday night soul mate evolve into something that strangely resembles a—gulp— relationship.

While it's true that many hookups become regular gigs (see "Are-You-My-Boyfriend?" on page 62), these nonrelationships usually stay within casual boundaries—meaning that neither party would ever think of uttering the word "boyfriend" or "girlfriend" aloud. Things continue along this same hazy road of booze and booty calls until it gets boring (you know it's over when you're thinking about how to perfect your Downward Dog while he's going down on you). Or maybe you meet someone who you click with both inside and outside the bar. Hookups fade all the time. Life goes on, ob-la-di, ob-la-da.

But let's say that you've been hooking up with someone on a regular basis (and no, that doesn't mean two Saturday nights in a row) and you're feeling really positive about the situation. He seems like he's really into you. For starters, you can't remember a time when he made a mad dash out the door the morning after hooking up, muttering, "I got shit to take care of—peace." He even knows that you prefer brown rice with your Chinese food, and you—well, you really like him.

While you've probably been involved with this type of habitual hookup before, this one feels a little different. If you can't quite put your finger on what separates him from the others, here are some indicators that you two may be sitting in a tree, K-I-S-S-I-N-G.

YOU LOSE YOUR PHONE PHOBIA

With just any old hookup, you adhere strictly to the rules of the phone game. But this time around, you don't wait for him to call you or make it a point to let a few days go by before you call him back. Instead, you feel confident enough to pick up the phone whenever you feel like it, whether it's just to say, "Hey, what's up?" or to let him know that his favorite episode of *The Simpsons* is on.

YOU LOOSEN UP AROUND HIM

You've finally moved past the point of turning on the water in the bathroom while you pee at his place, but at the same time it's not like you're ready to go with the door open. You're getting used to hanging out with him, and as a result, you let him see the "real you," meaning the girl who can pack away three Taco Bell burritos in one sitting, yet will only drink Diet Coke.

YOU HAVE SOBER HOOKUPS

By no means have the two of you stopped getting shitfaced together, but it's no longer a necessity to be ridiculously bombed every time you hook up. Once or twice a week you might actually grab just one drink and head back to your place to watch HBO.

And instead of his sleeping at your place merely because he's too intoxicated to find his way home, now he's all for having sober, school-night sleepovers.[24]

YOU DON'T DISH THE DIRT (AS MUCH)

When you're hooking up with a guy who sucks, usually your friends are forced to listen to every single little detail, from the dickhead thing he said at the bar to the asshole move he pulled the morning after. And like a good reality show, it's the drama that keeps the audience tuning in. On the other hand, when you're involved in a hookup that has the potential to be something more, there's just that much less shit to talk about him, which means that unless the girls want to sit around and hear about how things are going really well, it's likely that you will keep the play-by-play short and sweet.

---

[24] A sober hookup is not the same thing as when you get it on the morning after a drunken encounter.

MORE THAN WORDS
Having "The Talk"

If all of the previous factors are present, then you'd think it is safe to assume you two are headed straight toward coupledom. However, there is one crucial element missing here that can literally make or break your "relationship" and that's (cue the scary horror movie music): THE TALK.

Typically, the only topics that guys are willing to open up and express their true feelings about are limited to basketball, football, baseball—oh yeah, and their love for Pamela Anderson. But when it comes to discussing where they see a relationship going, they get quieter than a mime. What's a girl to do? Well, you could go for option A, which entails saying absolutely nothing to him but analyzing his actions for hours with your girlfriends, your manicurist, your coworkers, and so on. Then there's option B, the ever-popular we-have-to-talk approach, in which you completely accost your unsuspecting nonboyfriend and put him on the spot, only to watch him start sweating and mumbling incoherently.

We think it's probably ideal to go with option C: the "Faux Fight." Start an argument about something completely insignificant. Chances are, this fight will result in your feelings getting hurt and his feeling incredibly guilty about it (even though he doesn't know what the hell he did in the first place). Then the two of you will have a melodramatic heart-to-heart, in which he'll unknowingly fall right into the "what are we?" discussion. If it sounds passive-aggressive, that's because it is. [*Authors' note:* Just because you're getting him to talk doesn't mean you are going to like what he has to say (*"Yeah, I like hanging out with you, too—in bed."*), but at least you'll finally know where you stand and can proceed accordingly.]

If you still need some guidelines for getting your hookup to put it all out on the table, check out these life-saving tips.

THE DOS AND DON'TS OF INITIATING "THE TALK"

Do choose the right setting.

> *Don't think of setting only in terms of classic diamond solitaire versus princess cut.*

Do use "us" and "we" rather than "you" and "me."

> *Don't pretend that "we're" pregnant in order to bring "you and me" closer.*

Do wait until he is feeling relaxed before broaching the subject.

> *Don't offer him a couple of bong hits before you tell him you want to talk.*

Do find a nice quiet place where the two of you can be alone, without distractions.

> *Don't hit the childproof locks while he is riding shotgun in your car and vow that you are going to swerve into oncoming traffic unless he says he loves you.*

Do say something like, "I really like hanging out with you and would like to spend more time together."

> *Don't say, "I really like hanging out with you, and in order for us to spend more time together I've decided to move in with you."*

Do make sure that he wants to be your boyfriend before you introduce him as that to all of your friends.

> *Don't ask your best friend to "accidentally" introduce him as your boyfriend, then check out his expression to gauge what he thinks.*

Do respect his decision if he says that he doesn't really see a future with you.

> *Don't look him in the eye and say, "Ummm, I disagree" if he tells you that he doesn't see this going anywhere.*

Do tell him what you want from the relationship before you ask him what he wants.

> *Don't tell him that you want a June wedding because that's when your Vera Wang will be ready.*

STRANGER THINGS HAVE HAPPENED
Three True Tales from Hookup to Relationship

The fundamental difference between dating and hooking up can be summed up as follows: While dating, you have to do the whole getting-to-know-each-other thing before you make out or go home with him or do whatever you do, you nasty girl. You also have to make sure to look sexy but not slutty, arrive after he does but not so late that you seem flaky, and say intelligent things, but not so intelligent that you seem like you're trying too hard. It's no wonder most people equate the early stages of dating with interviewing for a job.

On the other hand, hooking up is the exact opposite. It's a lot less formal: You act purely on attraction (or how many drinks you've consumed) and just see where the tide takes you. If dating is a book, then think of hooking up as the book on tape, meaning that you still get most of the same things out of it, but in a much more entertaining, less time-consuming way.

This brings us to the most common misconception about hooking up. Many people think that if you make out with someone first and get to know them second, it's unlikely that you'll ever make it past a physical level. There's this notion that if you want a relationship, your options are limited to: (1) letting your mother set you up with the son of someone in her book club; (2) putting yourself on Match.com or JDate.com and hoping that he doesn't turn out to be short, bald, or some kind of Dungeons & Dragons freak; (3) sitting around looking pretty on a barstool and hoping that some fabulous guy will ask for your number and actually call you.

We're not saying that dating won't get you where you want to be romantically (hey, it worked for 50 percent of our parents), it's just that it's not the only way to get there. Why face another excruciating date where you are more into your pan-seared ahi tuna than the loser sitting across from you who's babbling on and on about his stock portfolio, when you can go out with your girls, get drunk and maybe, just maybe, make out with the cute friend of a friend? Hey, ya never know—that friend of a friend could turn out to be your boyfriend. If you don't believe us, check out these stories of girls who had a hookup turn into something way more substantial. These just reaffirm that freakin' annoying saying, "It'll happen when you least expect it." So go on and lower your expectations—the drinks are on us.[25]

JENNIFER AND JOSH
She Had Him at "Hello" (and the Fact That She Wasn't Wearing Any Underwear Didn't Hurt)

WHERE THEY MET: During the summer waiting in line for the bathroom at a bar

HER FIRST IMPRESSION OF HIM: She claims he was very cute and a great dresser, but admits that it was all sort of blurry due to the number of drinks she had consumed.

WHAT SHE WAS WEARING: A black sundress—no underwear (she says he still talks about it to this day).

WHAT SHE WAS DRINKING: The better question is, what wasn't she drinking?

---

[25] Okay, not really. But if we see you at a bar we'll totally get the next round.

HER ROMANTIC STATUS AT THE TIME: She had hooked up with another one of Josh's frat brothers the night before, but she wouldn't say they were "involved" at all. Ironically, that frat brother didn't speak to her for several months after she and Josh started dating.

HOW IT ALL WENT DOWN THE FIRST TIME THEY HOOKED UP: They got out of a cab in front of her apartment (conveniently, he lived three blocks away from her), and he asked if she wanted to go to his place and "watch a movie." Clearly impressed with his originality, she said yes. After talking for forty-five minutes, they started kissing, and then one thing led to another. Later on in the relationship, he told her that after that conversation he knew he was in love. Interestingly enough, she couldn't seem to remember a damn thing they talked about.

HER POST-HOOKUP THOUGHTS: "I'm going to throw up, I'm so drunk!"

WAS THERE A SLEEPOVER? Yup—they both passed out in his bed. He had plans to leave for the beach early the next morning, so when they woke up, all of his guy friends were on their way over to his apartment to pick him up and she booked it out of there.

WALK OF SHAME DETAILS: She was still wearing her sundress, still sans underwear. She had mascara all over her face and her hair looked like a bird's nest. Luckily she made it to her apartment without seeing anyone she knew.

HER EXPECTATIONS: Considering that she almost fainted when he asked for her phone number, she assumed that it was just a random drunk hookup.

WHAT MADE THIS HOOKUP DIFFERENT FROM ALL THE OTHERS: The fact that he actually called her the next day

WHAT HER FRIENDS SAID: On Passover people ask, "Why is this night different from all others?" That is what everyone said to Jennifer at the time, since she had been getting into the habit of drinking a lot and hooking up with random people.

THE MOMENT OF TRUTH: The first time they just hung out at his apartment and watched TV instead of going out, getting drunk, and hooking up, she knew it was the real thing.

HOW "THE TALK" HAPPENED: He ran into one of her friend's older sisters at a bar, and she introduced him as "Jen's boyfriend." He met up with her later on that night and said, "So, am I your boyfriend? Because your friend's sister just said that I was." Jen then said yes, and they filled out all the correct paperwork and received their couple card the following week in the mail.

JEN'S PARTING WORDS OF ADVICE: "Don't think that every hookup will lead to a relationship, because you will only end up getting hurt, but at the same time, don't think that every hookup won't lead to a relationship, because things happen when you are least expecting them to."

AUTHORS' NOTE: What Jen is trying to say is that you should think of it like that arcade game with the claw that picks up toys—you never expect to actually win anything, but every so often you surprise yourself and walk away with a stuffed SpongeBob doll. Score!

ALI AND JEFF
The Seven-Year Itch—
the Longest Hookup in History

WHERE THEY MET: The first time was Labor Day weekend in 1996 at a party at her house, but they really started talking the first day of school in first-period English class.

HER FIRST IMPRESSION OF HIM: Initially she thought he might be a little mean, because he had these intense, narrow green eyes, but then she was drawn to him because he had red hair and she had a thing for redheads. Overall, she loved the way he dressed and his whole mysterious aura.

WHAT SHE WAS WEARING: A black sleeveless short dress with a colorful little pattern of dots all over it, and patent leather chunky high-heel Mary Janes (this was the nineties)

WHAT SHE WAS DRINKING: Celestial Seasonings Cranberry Cove tea

HER ROMANTIC STATUS AT THE TIME: She wasn't involved with anyone, but he had been going out with a girl for about a year when they started hooking up.

HOW IT ALL WENT DOWN THE FIRST TIME THEY HOOKED UP: Since he had a girlfriend, they kept their operations covert.

WAS THERE A SLEEPOVER? No. It was a down-low kind of thing.

HER POST-HOOKUP THOUGHTS: She was thinking about how she could make it happen again.

WALK OF SHAME DETAILS: Not applicable, because of the whole "top-secret" element of the hookup.

HER EXPECTATIONS: Low, considering that he'd been with the same girl for a while. And since it seemed like they weren't going to break up, Ali decided to move on and start dating someone else, even though she still had a thing for him.

WHAT MADE THIS HOOKUP DIFFERENT FROM ALL THE OTHERS: It wasn't just lust-based. They had an intense mental and emotional connection.

WHAT HER FRIENDS SAID: They were totally behind it and helped her orchestrate situations where the two of them could be alone together.

THE MOMENT OF TRUTH: The moment didn't come for seven years. They kept hooking up sporadically during the entire course of their friendship. Then one night, he showed up at the hospital with flowers when she drove a needle through her foot on Thanksgiving (long story), after spending two hundred dollars on cabs to get there. Needless to say, she was smitten.

HOW "THE TALK" HAPPENED: They went out to dinner a couple of nights after the Thanksgiving debacle, and it was just obvious that they were totally together.

ALI'S PARTING WORDS OF ADVICE: "Don't ignore the thing right in front of your face. I mean, sometimes a hookup is just a hookup, but other times your body is a couple of steps ahead of your brain and your heart and just pulls you to someone because that's where you're supposed to be."

CAROLINE AND CHRIS
The Long-Distance Hookup

WHERE THEY MET: Chris was visiting from out of town and they got together at a mutual friend's birthday party.

HER FIRST IMPRESSION OF HIM: She thought he was cute.

WHAT SHE WAS WEARING: Jeans, a black top, and red stilettos, which she accessorized with a bag that he kept referring to as her "Grandma purse." (Actually, it was a very cute vintage handbag, thankyouverymuch, but what do guys know about timeless fashion, anyway?)

WHAT SHE WAS DRINKING: Vodka and all the shots he kept buying for her

HER ROMANTIC STATUS AT THE TIME: They were both hooking up with other people, who they obviously weren't very into.

HOW IT ALL WENT DOWN THE FIRST TIME THEY HOOKED UP: Toward the end of the evening, she was drunk and in need of a change of venue. Chris asked her, "So, what are you doing?" She replied, "I don't know what *you're* doing, but I'm going home." "Okay, I'm coming with you," he shot back.

So they went back to her apartment, talked for a bit, and then he tried out the I-need-to-shut-this-girl-up-by-kissing-her move. After some making out she told him, "I think you should probably go."

"Okay," he said, and then smiled coyly and took her by the hand into the bedroom. Caroline didn't protest, and the rest is history. (Cue Barry White music.)

WAS THERE A SLEEPOVER? Uh, obviously.

HER POST-HOOKUP THOUGHTS: Caroline was feeling a little torn about the situation—since she wasn't into spontaneous sleepovers with random boys she'd just met—and wondered if she had stepped into slut territory.

WALK OF SHAME DETAILS: Since she had played it perfectly and brought him back to her place, she didn't do any walking. Instead, he was the one who had to stumble out into the morning sunlight, feeling hungover and confused. After all, the hookup had completely blindsided him: He thought he was just going home with a cute blonde and (shock) he left actually liking her.

HER EXPECTATIONS: Part of her wished that something might come out of it, but Caroline didn't want to get her hopes up and then feel bad if nothing happened.

WHAT HER FRIENDS SAID: After it happened, Caroline's friends informed her that Chris had been kind of a dickhead in college. Plus, he lived a plane ride away from her, so no one wanted to give her false hope that a relationship would come out of the hookup.

THE MOMENT OF TRUTH: He came back a few weeks later, which happened to be Halloween weekend, and planned to meet up with her at a costume party. When they saw each other they just knew. And, oh yeah, Caroline was dressed as bridal Britney Spears (circa the Madonna make-out at the MTV Video Music Awards, as opposed to the quickie nuptials in Vegas—not that it made a difference to Chris).

HOW "THE TALK" HAPPENED: It didn't, really. They started talking every day and he invited her to his company Christmas party. Somewhere between the long-distance phone calls and biweekly flights to visit each other, they became an official couple. Word on the street is that Chris quit his job and is apartment hunting in Caroline's neck of the woods. . . .

WHAT MADE THIS HOOKUP DIFFERENT FROM ALL THE OTHERS? Until meeting Chris, all of Caroline's hookups had a six-week expiration date.

CAROLINE'S PARTING WORDS OF ADVICE:[26] Caroline says, "Don't be a chicken. If it feels right, go for it."

---

[26] Some helpful advice from Caroline's boyfriend: "Always wear clean underwear, never eat yellow snow, and do whatever Ed McMahon used to say at the end of *Star Search.* I think it was 'Reach for the Stars.'"

LAST CALL
You Don't Have to Go Home with Him, but You Can't Stay Here

I f you've ever sat home alone on the couch and devoured an entire roll of chocolate chip cookie dough while watching *The Fabulous Life of . . . Christina Aguilera* for the hundredth time, you've probably felt a little pathetic (we've all been there). Now picture this: You and your best friends skip into the supermarket, charge right for the cookie dough, and giggle with anticipation about how fun it'll be to go home and eat the whole roll while watching cheesy TV shows together. That's a party.

Maybe we all should approach hooking up in the same manner: Rather than thinking of it as a lonely, guilty thing, we should use it as a chance to bond with our closest buds and live single life to the absolute fullest. We are merely building up a collection of the good, the bad, and the ugly to pull out at a later date, share with our friends over cocktails, and never forget that we are young, fabulous, and a hell of a lot more fun than those girls who jump from one attached-at-the-hip relationship to another.

ALL WE REALLY NEED TO KNOW WE LEARNED FROM HOOKING UP
(Well, Maybe Not Quite, But . . .)

- Three hookups do not a boyfriend make.

- Girls break hearts too.

- Guy friends are great for hanging out with but usually make for a hookup disaster (unless, of course, you get magically beamed up into a Meg Ryan movie).

- Yes, he really was as painfully boring as your friends kept telling you.

- No, he doesn't want to know about your family—not even your sweet old nana and all the funny things she says.

- Wearing sweatpants in front of your hookup is the quickest way to end things.

- When some stupid boy gives you the pink slip and leaves you feeling down in the dumps, just remember: This too shall pass. (Oh, and one day, he'll be sporting a comb-over and nose hair.)

- When you spend hours analyzing the state of the hookup with your friends, dissecting everything he's ever said or done, and even creating a Powerpoint presentation that will attempt to answer the question, "What is he thinking?," just know that the answer is always NOTHING. He isn't thinking about it AT ALL—nope, not even one bit.

- If you are only hooking up with someone out of boredom, maybe you should take up knitting, tai chi, or pilates until someone more interesting comes along.

- While it's okay to stop hooking up in order to pursue a real relationship, always remember: Once you are part of a couple, your morning-after brunch stories will be significantly less entertaining.

- Know when to set him free: A little drama in your life is fun, but too much is a Lifetime movie.

- Your mother never had this much fun.